Microsoft® Office 98

Macintosh® Edition

At a Glance

Microsoft®*Press*

Microsoft Office 98 Macintosh Edition At a Glance

Published by **Microsoft Press**
A Division of Microsoft Corporation
One Microsoft Way
Redmond, Washington 98052-6399

Library of Congress Cataloging-in-Publication Data
Microsoft Office 98 Macintosh Edition At a Glance / Perspection, Inc.
     p.   cm.
  Includes index.
  ISBN 1-57231-916-X
  1. Microsoft Office. 2. Microsoft Word. 3. Microsoft Excel 4. Microsoft PowerPoint. 5. Business--Computer programs.
  6. Word processing. 7. Electronic spreadsheets. 8. Business presentations--Graphic methods--Computer programs.
  I. Perspection, Inc.
HF5548.4.M525M5247   1998
005.369--dc21   98-9351
                                     CIP

Printed and bound in the United States of America.

1 2 3 4 5 6 7 8 9 QEQE 3 2 1 0 9 8

Distributed to the book trade in Canada by Macmillan of Canada, a division of Canada Publishing Corporation.

A CIP catalogue record for this book is available from the British Library.

Microsoft Press books are available through booksellers and distributors worldwide. For further information about international editions, contact your local Microsoft Corporation office. Or contact Microsoft Press International directly at fax (425) 936-7329. Visit our Web site at mspress.microsoft.com.

For Perspection, Inc.
Writer: **Steven M. Johnson**
Production Editor: **David W. Beskeen**
Series and Developmental Editor: **Jane Pedicini**
Technical Editor: **Nicholas Chu**

For Microsoft Press
Acquisitions Editor: **Kim Fryer**
Project Editor: **Maureen Williams Zimmerman**

Contents

"How can I get started quickly in Office 98?"

see page 6

Get help with the
Office Assistant
see page 16

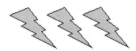

Draw and enhance objects
see page 38

Use a hyperlink
see page 45

Use Internet Explorer
to browse Web pages
see page 62

*"How can I view
my documents
effectively in
Word?"*

see page 65

A B C

Format text for emphasis
see page 82

Learn to use styles
see page 95

*"How can I track
changes made in
my document?"*

see page 111

"How can I create a worksheet?"

see page 126

"I want to create a formula!"

see page 140

Create a chart
see page 150

Create links between worksheets
see page 176

"How can record and run a macro?"

see pages 181-182

Create a new presentation
see page 184

Insert a chart in a slide
see page 206

Create a slide transition
in PowerPoint
see page 210

Send a file attached to
an E-mail message
see page 232

About
At a Glance

Microsoft Office 98 Macintosh Edition At a Glance is for anyone who wants to get the most from their computer and their software with the least amount of time and effort. You'll find this book to be a straightforward, easy-to-read reference tool. With the premise that your computer should work for you, not you for it, this book's purpose is to help you get your work done quickly and efficiently so that you can get away from the computer and live your life.

No Computerese!

Let's face it—when there's a task you don't know how to do but you need to get it done in a hurry, or when you're stuck in the middle of a task and can't figure out what to do next, there's nothing more frustrating than having to read page after page of technical background material. You want the information you need—nothing more, nothing less—and you want it now! And it should be easy to find and understand.

That's what this book is all about. It's written in plain English—no technical jargon and no computerese. There's no single task in the book that takes more than two pages. Just look up the task in the index or the table of contents, turn to the page, and there's the information, laid out step by step and accompanied by a graphic that adds visual clarity. You don't get bogged down by the whys and wherefores; just follow the steps, look at the illustrations, and get your work done with a minimum of hassle.

Occasionally you might want to turn to another page if the procedure you're working on has a "See Also" in the left column. That's because there's a lot of overlap among tasks, and we didn't want to keep repeating ourselves. We've also scattered some useful tips here and there, and thrown in a "Try This" once in a while, but by and large we've tried to remain true to the heart and soul of the book, which is that information you need should be available to you at a glance.

Useful Tasks...

Whether you use Office 98 Macintosh Edition for work, play, or some of each, we've tried to pack this book with procedures for everything we could think of that you might want to do, from the simplest tasks to some of the more esoteric ones.

...And the Easiest Way to Do Them

Another thing we've tried to do in *Office 98 Macintosh Edition At a Glance* is to find and document the easiest way to accomplish a task. Office often provides many ways to accomplish a single end result, which can be daunting or delightful, depending on the way you like to work. If you tend to stick with one favorite and familiar approach, we think the methods described in this book are the way to go. If you like trying out alternative techniques, go ahead! The intuitiveness of Office invites exploration, and you're likely to discover ways of doing things that you think are easier or that you like better. If you do, that's great! It's exactly what the creators of Office 98 Macintosh Edition had in mind when they provided so many alternatives.

A Quick Overview

This book isn't meant to be read in any particular order. It's designed so that you can jump in, get the information you need, and then close the book and keep it near your computer until the next time you need it. But that doesn't mean we scattered the information about with wild abandon. If you were to read the book from front to back, you'd find a logical progression from the simple tasks to the more complex ones. Here's a quick overview.

Sections 2 and 3 of the book cover the basics: starting Microsoft Office 98 Macintosh programs; working with menus, toolbars, and dialog boxes; getting help; creating and opening files; editing your text; making corrections; saving documents; closing documents; and exiting programs.

Section 4 describes tasks for exploring the Internet with Office 98 programs: inserting and using hyperlinks; navigating hyperlinks, searching the Web; creating and saving documents for the Web; and previewing Web pages from your computer or the Internet.

Sections 5 through 7 describe tasks for creating documents with Microsoft Word: changing document views; formatting text for emphasis; creating form letters; creating and modifying tables; adding desktop publishing effects, checking your spelling, grammar, and word usage; and printing documents.

Sections 8 through 10 describe tasks for creating spreadsheets with Microsoft Excel: entering labels and numbers; creating formulas; creating charts, lists, and PivotTables; creating and modifying templates; consolidating data; creating "what-if" scenarios; generating multiple page reports; and recording and running macros.

Sections 11 and 12 describe tasks for creating presentations with Microsoft PowerPoint: creating a new presentation; developing an outline; preparing speaker notes and handouts; adding a header and footer; inserting slides, charts, clip art, pictures, sounds, and movies; applying color schemes and animations; and creating slide shows.

Section 13 describes tasks for integrating information from Office 98 programs: sharing information between programs; embedding and linking files between programs; publishing and subscribing to an edition; creating Word documents with Excel data; creating PowerPoint presentations with Word text; sending files in e-mail messages; and exchanging messages using Outlook Express.

A Final Word (or Two)

We had three goals in writing this book, and here they are:

◆ Whatever you want to do, we want the book to help you get it done.

◆ We want the book to help you discover how to do things you *didn't* know you wanted to do.

◆ And, finally, we want the book to help you enjoy doing your work with Office 98.

We hope you'll have as much fun using *Office 98 Macintosh Edition At a Glance* as we've had writing it. If you have any comments or suggestions regarding this book, visit our Web site at www.perspection.com. The best way to learn is by doing, and that's what we hope you'll get from this book.

Jump right in!

Getting Started with Office 98

Microsoft Office 98 is simple to use so you can focus on the important challenge—your work. What's more, all the Office 98 Macintosh programs—Word, Excel, and PowerPoint—function alike in many ways.

Working Efficiently with Office 98

Every Office 98 program contains several identical commands and buttons, which allow you to perform basic actions the same way, no matter which program you happen to be working in. For example, when you click the Open button on the Standard toolbar in Word, Excel, or PowerPoint, the same Open dialog box appears. Similarly, the Close box for any document window in Office 98 is identical.

In Office 98, you can perform many common tasks in several different ways. The method you choose depends on your personal preference. For example, suppose you need to start a program and open a document. You could start the program first and then open the file from within the program. Or you could open the file and its associated program at the same time. The choice is yours.

Installing Office 98

To take advantage of the latest Apple technologies, Microsoft Office 98 for the Macintosh is designed to run on PowerPC-based computers using the Mac OS 8.0 or later. Drag-and-drop installation makes it easy to set up and manage Office 98. You simply drag the Microsoft Office 98 folder from the Microsoft Office 98 CD-ROM to a local hard or network drive. Office 98 also enables you to customize installations to meet unique requirements. You can also install Office 98 program enhancements and components from the Value Pack. Although not part of the standard installation, you can also install Microsoft Internet solutions: Outlook Express (an Internet e-mail program) and Internet Explorer (an Internet browser).

Install Office 98 Using Drag-and-Drop

1. Insert the Microsoft Office 98 CD-ROM into the CD-ROM drive.

2. Double-click the Microsoft Office 98 icon, if necessary.

3. Drag the Microsoft Office 98 folder icon to the hard drive icon on the Desktop.

   In this case, the hard drive icon is called Macintosh HD.

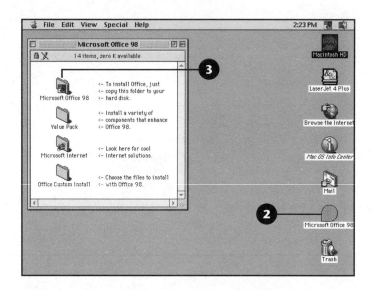

Install Office 98 Using the Custom Installer

1. Insert the Microsoft Office 98 CD-ROM into the CD-ROM drive.

2. Double-click the Office Custom Install folder.

3. Double-click the Microsoft Office Installer icon.

4. Click the pop-up menu, and then select Custom Install.

5. Click the component check boxes that you want to install.

6. Click Install.

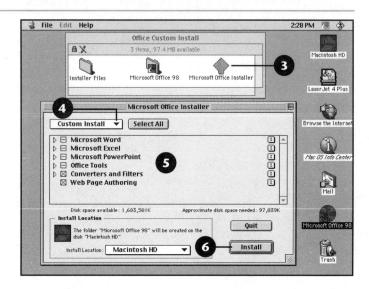

Install components from the Value Pack. *The Value Pack located on the Microsoft Office 98 CD-ROM provides you with utilities, tools, and files to help you use Office 98 more efficiently and effectively. Check it out!*

Value Pack Installer icon

Self-repairing programs. *If you change the name of your hard drive, drag folders to new locations, or clean out the system Extensions folder, Office 98 programs detect the changes, and then replace files and change settings.*

Uninstall Office 98 or previous Office versions. *The Microsoft Office Installer can remove Office 98 or a previous version from a local or network drive, regardless of how Office was initially installed.*

Install Components from the Value Pack

1. Insert the Microsoft Office 98 CD-ROM into the CD-ROM drive.

2. Double-click the Value Pack folder.

3. Double-click the Value Pack Installer icon.

4. Click the component check boxes that you want to install.

5. Click Install.

Scroll to view other available components.

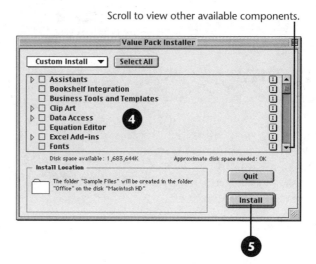

Install Microsoft Internet Solutions

1. Insert the Microsoft Office 98 CD-ROM into the CD-ROM drive.

2. Double-click the Microsoft Internet folder.

3. Double-click the Installer icon for the Microsoft Internet solution you want to install.

4. Click Accept to the license agreement.

5. Click Install.

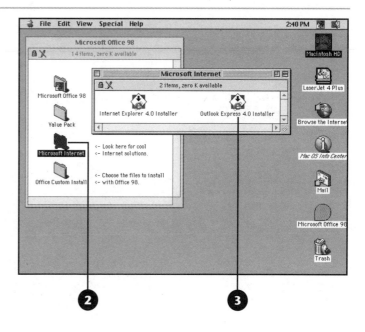

Starting an Office 98 Program

All Office 98 programs start in the same two ways: either from the Microsoft Office 98 folder on your hard drive or from the Office Manager. The Office Manager is probably more convenient because it saves a few mouse clicks. By providing different ways to start a program, Office 98 enables you to customize the way you work and to switch from program to program with a click of a button.

Microsoft Office 98 icon

TIP

Install the Office Manager. *Insert the Microsoft Office 98 CD-ROM, open the Value Pack folder, double-click the Value Pack Installer, click the Microsoft Office Manager check box, and then click Install.*

Start an Office 98 Program from the Desktop

1 Double-click the hard drive icon on the Desktop with the Office 98 folder.

2 Double-click the Microsoft Office 98 folder icon.

3 Double-click the Office 98 program icon you want to open.

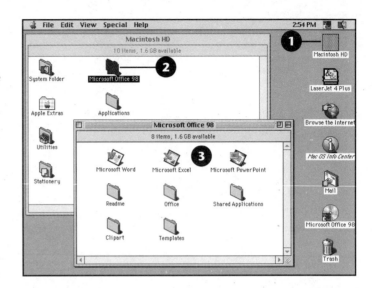

Start an Office 98 Program Using the Office Manager

1 Click the Office Manager icon on the Desktop menu bar.

2 Click the Office 98 program icon you want to start.

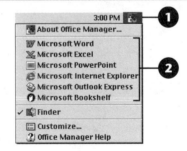

Creating a New File

There are two common ways to create a new file: start an Office 98 program or choose the New command from within an Office 98 program. When you start an Office 98 program, a program window opens, displaying a blank document or a wizard. A wizard helps you get started. From within an Office 98 program, you can choose the New command, and then select a document style to create a new file. The Office 98 programs provide you with a variety of document styles to choose from to help you create a new file.

SEE ALSO

See "Choosing Templates or Wizards" on page 26 for information on choosing a document style from the New dialog box.

Create a New File from the Desktop

(1) Double-click the hard drive icon on the Desktop with the Office 98 folder.

(2) Double-click the Microsoft Office 98 folder icon.

(3) Double-click the Office 98 program icon you want to open.

A program window opens, displaying a blank document or a dialog box.

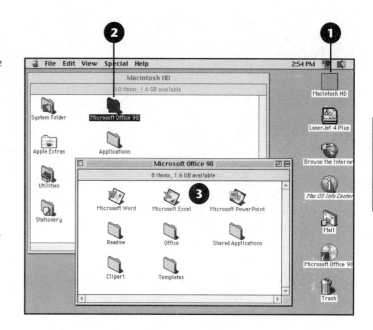

Create a New File from Within a Program

(1) Click the File menu, and then click New.

(2) Click the tab for the type of document you want to create.

(3) Click the Document option button.

(4) Click a document style.

(5) Click OK.

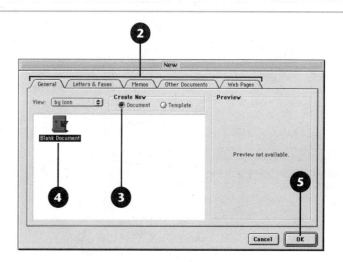

Opening an Existing File

Before you can begin working, you need to open a document to work on. There are two common ways to open an existing file: open the file and the program in which it was created at one time, or open the file from within its Office 98 program. If you have difficulty remembering where or under what name you stored a particular file, you can locate the file using the Find File option in the Open dialog box.

Open button

TIP

Use the File menu to open a recent file. *You can open any of the four most recent files on which you worked in any Office program by clicking the appropriate filename at the bottom of the File menu.*

Open an Existing File from the Desktop

1 Double-click the hard drive icon in which the file is stored.

2 Double-click the folder in which the file is stored.

3 Double-click a filename to start the program and open that file.

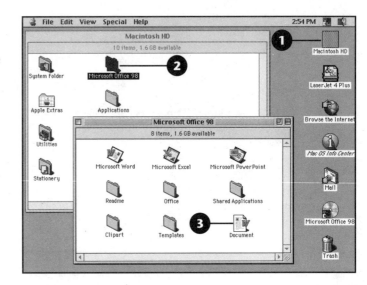

Open an Existing File from Within a Program

1 Click the Open button on the Standard toolbar.

2 Click the Select A Document pop-up menu, and then select the drive where the file is located.

3 If necessary, double-click the folder in which the file is stored.

4 Click the List Files Of Type pop-up menu, and then select the type of file you want to open.

5 Double-click the file you want to open.

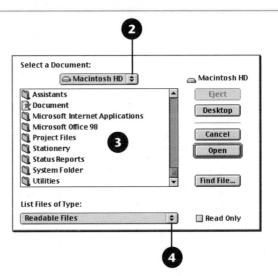

TIP

Use Advanced Search to find files. *In the Search dialog box, you can click the Advanced Search button to find files by document summary information or the creation or last saved date.*

SEE ALSO

See "Choosing Menu and Dialog Box Options" on page 22 for information about using dialog boxes.

TIP

Open Office 97 files for Windows and NT. *Office 98 for the Macintosh is 100% compatible with Office 97 for Windows and NT. To open an Office 97 file, transfer the file to the Macintosh, start the Office 98 program, click the File menu, click Open, click the List Files Of Type pop-up menu, select All Files, select the file you want to open, then click Open.*

Find a File Quickly Using the Open Dialog Box

1 Click the Open button on the Standard toolbar.

2 Click Find File.

3 Enter the name of the file you want to find.

4 Click the File Type pop-up menu, and then select the file type you want to find.

5 Click the Location pop-up menu, and then select the drive you want to search.

6 Click Save Search As, enter a search name, and then click OK to save the search criteria (optional).

7 Click OK.

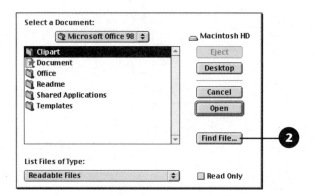

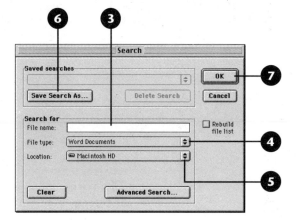

Saving a File

Saving your files frequently ensures you don't lose work in case of an unexpected power loss. The first time you save, you must specify a filename and folder in the Save As dialog box. The next time you save, Office saves the file with the same name in the same folder. If you want to change a file's name or save it in a new folder, you must use the Save As dialog box again, which actually creates a copy of the original file. If you haven't saved your work before you close a file, a dialog box opens, asking if you want to save your changes.

Save a File for the First Time

1. Click the Save button on the Standard toolbar.

2. Click the pop-up menu, and then select the drive where you want to save the file.

3. Double-click the folder in which you want to save the file.

4. Type a name for the file, or use the suggested name.

5. Click Save.

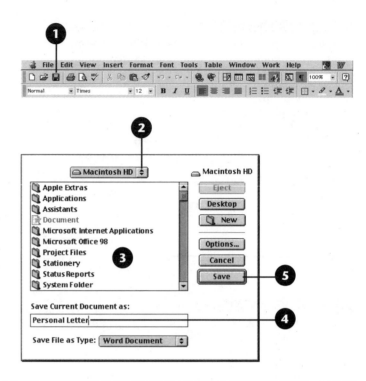

Save a File with Another Name

1. Click the File menu, and then click Save As.

2. Type a new name for the file.

3. Click Save.

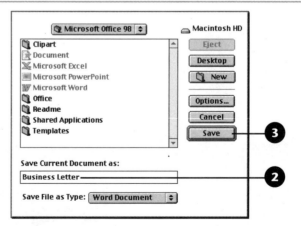

TIP

Use Save Options to create a backup copy of a file.

Click the File menu, click Save As, click Options, click the Always Create Backup Copy check box, and then click OK. When you save a file, a backup copy is automatically saved.

TIP

Use file types to save a file.

A file type specifies the document format (for example, a template) and the program version in which a file was created (for example, Word 7.0). You might want to change the document format or program and version if you're sharing files with someone who has an earlier version of a program or is working with Office 97 for Windows.

SEE ALSO

See "Importing and Exporting Files" on page 222 for more information about saving a document as another file type.

Save a File in a Different Folder

(1) Click the File menu, and then click Save As.

(2) Click the pop-up menu, and then select the drive where you want to save the file.

(3) Double-click the folder in which you want to save the file.

(4) Click Save.

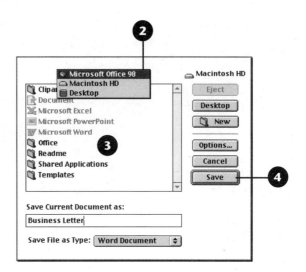

Save a File as a Different Type

(1) Click the File menu, and then click Save As.

(2) Click the Save File As Type pop-up menu, and then select the file type you want.

(3) Click Save.

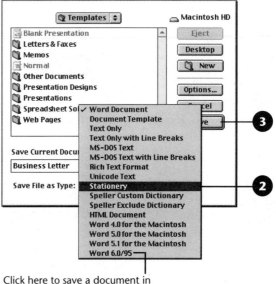

Click here to save a document in Word for Windows 95 format.

Getting Help in an Office 98 Program

At some point, everyone has a question or two about the program they are using. Office 98's online Help system provides the answers you need. With *balloon help*, you are a mouse-pointer away whenever you want information about anything you see on the screen or in a dialog box. You can get balloon help by clicking the Help menu and then click Show Balloons. In addition, you can also search an extensive catalog of Help topics to locate general or specific information.

Locate Information with Balloon Help

1 Click the Help menu, and then click Show Balloons.

2 Point to items on the screen that you want more information about.

3 When you are finished, click the Help menu, and then click Hide Balloons.

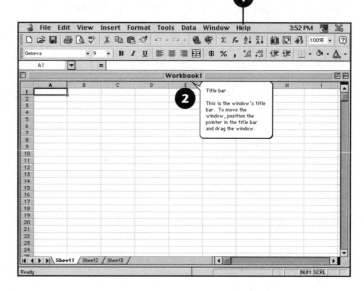

Locate Information from the Table of Contents

1 Click the Help menu, and then click Contents And Index.

2 Click a topic that relates most closely to the information you want.

3 Click a subtopic to find the information you want.

4 When you are finished, click the Close box on the Help window.

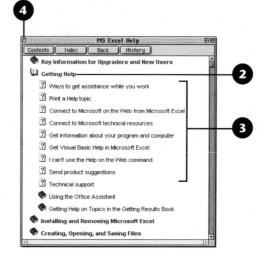

SEE ALSO

See "Getting Help from the Office Assistant" on page 16 for information about finding out how to accomplish a certain task.

TRY THIS

Get information about the Web. In every Office 98 program, you can get information about the World Wide Web. Click the Help menu, and then click Help On The Web.

Locate Information about a Particular Topic

(**1**) Click the Help menu, and then click Contents And Index.

(**2**) Click the Index button.

(**3**) Type a word about which you want more information. As you type each letter of the word or topic, the topics list scrolls.

(**4**) Click a topic from the list that relates most closely to the information you want, and then click Show Topics.

(**5**) Click a specific topic, and then click Go To.

(**6**) After reading the Help window, click the Close box on the Help window.

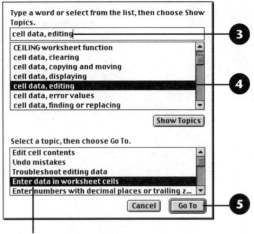

Click a specific topic here.

Click to look up another topic.

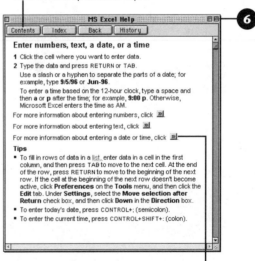

Click to display another Help window.

Getting Help from the Office Assistant

Often the easiest way to learn how to accomplish a certain task is to ask someone who knows. Now, with Office 98, that knowledgeable friend is always available in the form of the Office Assistant. You just tell the Assistant what you want to do in everyday language, and the Assistant walks you through the process step by step. And if Max's personality doesn't appeal to you, you can choose from a variety of other Assistants.

Office Assistant button

Ask the Office Assistant for Help

(1) Click the Office Assistant button on the Standard toolbar, or click the open Office Assistant window.

(2) Type the task you need help with in the box.

(3) Click Search.

(4) Click the topic you want help with.

(5) After you're done, click the Close box on the Help window.

(6) Click the Close box on the Office Assistant window.

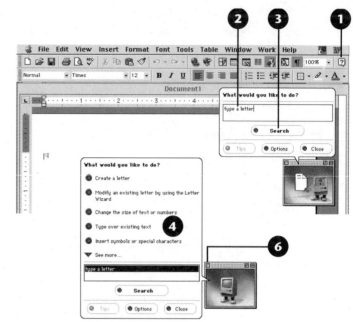

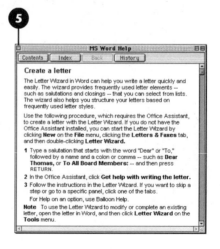

Max:
an Office Assistant

Choose an Assistant

1. Click the Office Assistant button on the Standard toolbar.

2. Click Options.

3. Click the Gallery tab.

4. Click the Next and Back buttons to preview different Assistants.

5. Leave the Assistant you want to use visible.

6. Click OK.

Change Office Assistant Options

1. Click the Office Assistant button on the Standard toolbar.

2. Click Options.

3. Click the Options tab.

4. Click the check boxes with the Office Assistant options you want to turn on or off.

5. Click OK.

Use this tab to customize the Office Assistant with more advanced features.

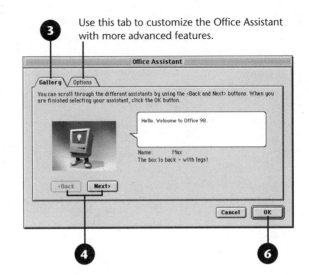

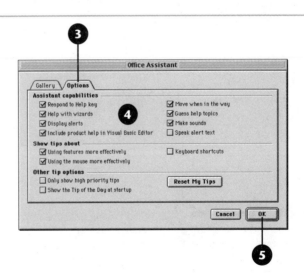

Working with Windows

Every Office program opens with a *document window*, where you create and edit your various documents. In most situations, you'll probably have only one window filling the entire screen at once. But when moving or copying information between windows, it's sometimes easier to see several windows at once.

SEE ALSO

See "Working with Multiple Documents" on page 68 for information on viewing multiple document windows within a program.

TIP

Create a duplicate window. *Click the Window menu, and then click New Window to create a copy of the active window.*

Resize and Move a Window

Use sizing boxes or the mouse pointer to resize and move the document window:

◆ Zoom box

   Click to make a window fill the entire screen. Click again to return the window to its original size.

◆ Collapse box/Expand box

   Click to hide a window leaving the title bar. Click again to show the window.

◆ Mouse pointer

   Drag a window's borders to resize it, or drag a title bar to move it.

Active window · Zoom box · Collapse box/Expand box

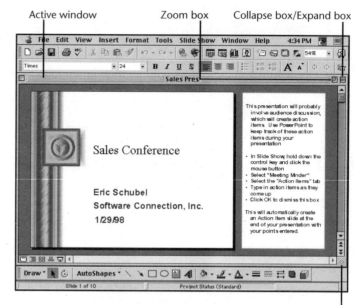

Drag to resize the window.

Arrange Multiple Open Windows

(1) Click the Window menu and then click Arrange All, or Arrange (for Excel).

   All the open document windows resize to fill the entire screen.

(2) Click the Window menu, and then click the document you want to work on, or click in the window (becomes the active window).

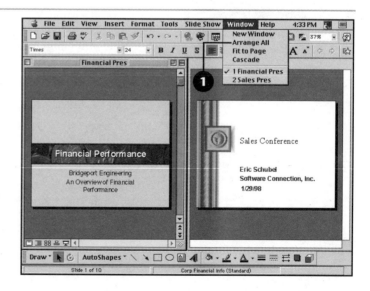

Closing a File

When you finish working on a file but do not want to exit the Office 98 program, you can close the file and then work on another file. If you try to close a document without saving your final changes, a dialog box appears, asking if you would like to do so.

Close box

SEE ALSO

See "Saving a File" on page 12 for information on saving changes to your documents.

Close a File

1. Click the File menu and then click Close, or click the Close box on the document window title bar.

2. If necessary, click Save to save your changes.

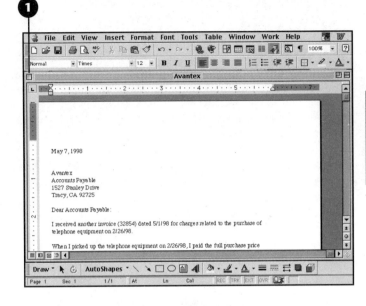

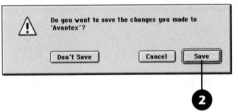

Quitting an Office 98 Program

When you finally decide to stop working for the day, the last things you need to do are close any documents that are open and close any programs that are running. You can close each document and its program separately. Or you can close everything at once by quitting the program. Either way, if you try to close a document without saving your final changes, a dialog box appears, asking if you would like to do so.

SEE ALSO

See "Closing a File" on page 19 for information on closing a document.

TIP

Hide a program. *Instead of quitting a program temporarily, hide the program and then display it when you want. Click the Application menu, and then select the program you want to hide.*

Quit an Office 98 Program

1 Click the File menu, and then click Quit.

2 If necessary, click Save to save any changes you made to your open documents before the program quits.

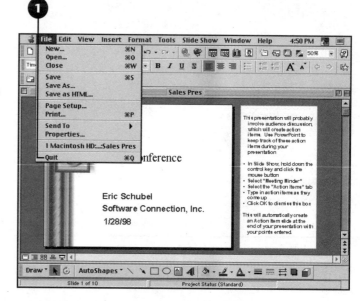

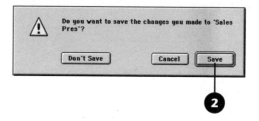

3

Using Shared Office 98 Tools

The great advantage of the many programs that make up Microsoft Office 98 is that they're designed to work together to allow you to focus on *what* you need to do, rather than *how*.

Similar Look and Function

When you start an Office 98 program, a document window opens, which contains a menu bar (access to the program's commands) and several toolbars (with buttons for the most commonly used commands). In this document window, you can create spreadsheets, letters, presentations, or reports, depending on the program. Each document window also contains sizing boxes (which allow you to resize the document window instantly).

Once you learn to use menus, toolbars, dialog boxes, and sizing boxes in one Office 98 program, you can apply the same techniques to all other Office programs. If you perform a task one way in Word 98, you probably already know how to perform the task in Excel 98 or PowerPoint 98. Go ahead and give it a try!

Choosing Menu and Dialog Box Options

A *menu* is a list of related commands. For example, an Edit menu contains commands for editing a document, such as Delete and Cut. A *shortcut menu* opens right where you're working and contains commands related to a specific object. Clicking a menu command that is followed by an ellipsis opens a *dialog box*, where you choose various options and settings and provide necessary information for completing the command. As you switch between programs, you'll find that all Office menus and dialog boxes look similar and work in the same way.

Choose Menu Commands

(1) Click a menu name on the menu bar at the top of the program window, or hold down the Control key and click an object (such as a toolbar, spreadsheet cell, picture, or selected text).

(2) If the menu command you want is followed by an arrow, point to it to open a submenu of related commands.

(3) Click a menu command to choose that command or to open a dialog box.

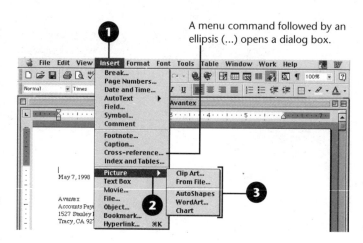

A menu command followed by an ellipsis (...) opens a dialog box.

Choose Dialog Box Options

An Office 98 dialog box can be extremely simple with only a few options or very complex with several sets of options on different tabs. Regardless of the number of choices, all dialog boxes look similar and use the same types of buttons, boxes, and lists, including:

◆ Tab. Each tab groups a related set of options. Click a tab to display its options.

◆ Option button. Click an option button to select it. You can usually select only one.

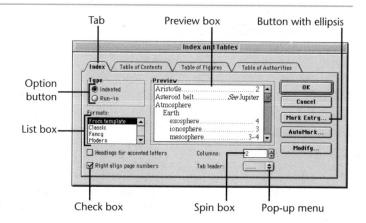

◆ Check box. Click the check box to turn the option on or off. A check means the option is selected; a cleared box means it's not.

◆ Spin box. Use this box to specify a value by clicking the up or down arrow to increase or decrease the number, or by typing the number you want in the box.

◆ Pop-up menu. The menu contains a preset list of options. Click the pop-up menu to display the list, and then select the option you want. You might need to scroll to see all the available options.

◆ Text box. Click in the box, and then type the specified information (such as a filename).

◆ Preview box. Many dialog boxes contain an image that changes to reflect the options you select.

◆ Button. Click a button to perform a specific action or command. The most common button is the OK button, which confirms your selections and closes the dialog box. When you click a button whose name is followed by an ellipsis (...), another dialog box opens.

Several dialog boxes require you to select a file or folder. Click the pop-up menu, and then select from a list of drives and folders on your computer.

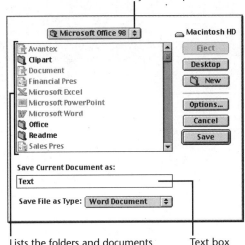

Lists the folders and documents available in the selected drive or folder. Double-click the one you want to open.

Text box

Working with Toolbars

Office 98 *toolbars* give you quick access to frequently used menu commands with the click of a button. Most programs open with a Standard toolbar (with commands like Save and Print) and a Formatting toolbar (with commands for selecting fonts and sizes). You can also display toolbars designed for specific tasks, such as drawing pictures, importing data, or creating charts, as necessary.

> **TIP**
>
> **Displaying the name of the toolbar button.** *To find out the name of a toolbar button, position the pointer over the button on the toolbar. The name of the button, or ScreenTip, appears below the button.*

Display and Hide a Toolbar

(1) Click the View menu, and then point to Toolbars.

(2) Click the name of the toolbar you want to display or hide.

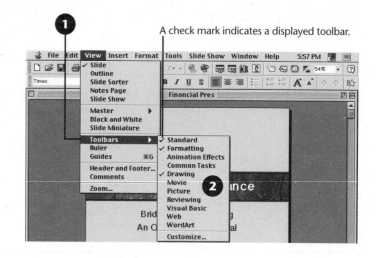

A check mark indicates a displayed toolbar.

Move and Resize a Toolbar

◆ To move a *docked* (attached to one edge of the program) toolbar to a floating location, double-click or drag the gray bar on the left edge of the toolbar.

◆ To move a *floating* (unattached) toolbar, click its title bar and drag it to a new location.

◆ To change the size or shape of a floating toolbar, drag any border until the toolbar is the shape you want.

◆ To return a floating toolbar to a docked location, drag its title bar to an edge of the program.

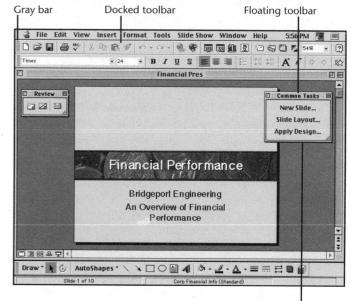

Gray bar   Docked toolbar   Floating toolbar

Drag the border to reshape a floating toolbar.

Hide ScreenTips. *To hide ScreenTips, click the View menu, point to Toolbars, click Customize, click the Options tab, clear the Show ScreenTips On Toolbars check box, and then click OK.*

Add the Shortcut Menus toolbar. *Click the View menu, point to Toolbars, click Customize, click the Toolbars tab, click the Shortcut Menus check box, and then click Close.*

Customize a Toolbar

(**1**) Click the View menu, point to Toolbars, and then click Customize.

(**2**) If the toolbar you want to customize is not displayed, click the Toolbars tab, and then click the appropriate check box to select it.

(**3**) Click the Commands tab.

(**4**) To add a button to a toolbar, click the type of button you want to add in the Categories box, and then drag a button from the Commands box to the toolbar where you want it to appear.

(**5**) To move a button, drag it to a new location on any visible toolbar.

(**6**) To remove a button from a toolbar, drag it off the toolbar.

(**7**) When you're done, click Close.

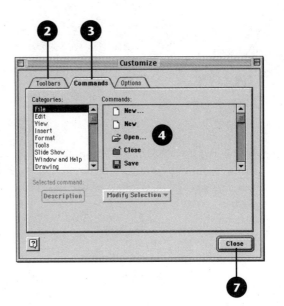

Choosing Templates and Wizards

Office 98 makes it easy to create many common documents based on a template or using a wizard. A *template* opens a document (such as a letter) with predefined formatting and placeholder text specifying what information you should enter (such as your address). A *wizard* walks you through the steps to create a finished document by asking you for information first. When you click Finish, the wizard creates a completely formatted document with the text you entered.

TRY THIS

Create your own letterhead. *Try using the Memo Wizard to create a professional-style interoffice memo or personal letterhead.*

Choose a Template

1. Start an Office program, click the File menu, and then click New.

2. Click the tab for the type of document you want to create, such as a letter.

3. Click the template you want to use.

4. Check the Preview box to make sure the template will create the right style of document.

5. Click OK.

6. Type text for placeholders such as "[Click here and type your letter text]" as indicated.

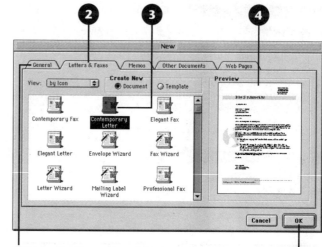

Contains the Normal templates to create a blank document in any Office program

Choose and Navigate a Wizard

1 Start an Office program, click the File menu, and then click New.

2 Click the tab for the type of document you want to create.

3 Double-click a wizard icon you want to use.

4 Read and select options (if necessary) in the first wizard dialog box.

5 Click Next to move to the next wizard dialog box.

Each wizard dialog box asks for different types of information.

6 Select the options you want, and then click Next.

7 When you reach the last wizard dialog box, click Finish.

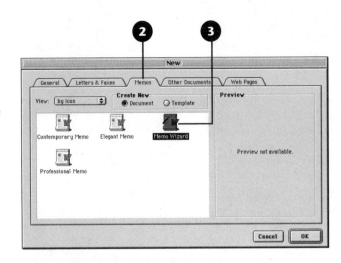

Fill in the necessary information.

Editing Your Text

Before you can edit your text, you need to highlight, or select, the text you want to work with. Once you select the text, you can delete or replace it. You can also move (*cut*) or *copy* text within one document or between documents in different programs. In either case, the steps are the same. The text is stored on the *Clipboard*, a temporary storage area, until you cut or copy a new selection. You can also move or copy selected text to a new location without storing it on the Clipboard using a technique called *drag-and-drop* editing.

SEE ALSO

See "Working with Windows" on page 18 for information on how to open and display multiple windows.

SEE ALSO

See "Selecting Text" on page 71 for more information on ways to select and edit your text.

Select and Edit Text

1 Position the pointer to the left or right of the text you want to select, and then click.

You can press the Delete or Del key to remove individual characters.

2 Drag the pointer to highlight the text you want to select.

3 Type to replace the selected text or press the Delete or Del key.

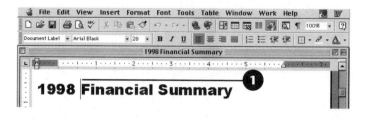

Cut or Copy and Paste Text

1 Select the text you want to move or copy.

2 Click the Cut or Copy button on the Standard toolbar.

3 Click where you want to insert the text.

4 Click the Paste button on the Standard toolbar.

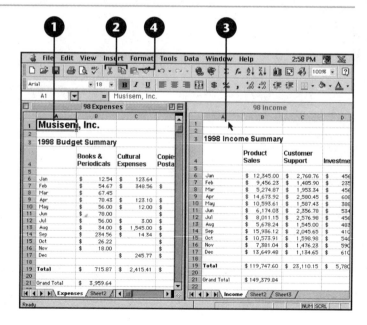

Drag and Drop Text

(1) If you want to drag and drop text between documents, display both document windows.

(2) Select the text you want to move or copy.

(3) To move the text to a new location, position the pointer over the selected text and then press and hold the mouse button.

(4) To copy the text and paste the copy in a new location, also press and hold the Option key.

(5) Drag the pointer to the new location.

(6) Release the mouse button (and the Option key, if necessary).

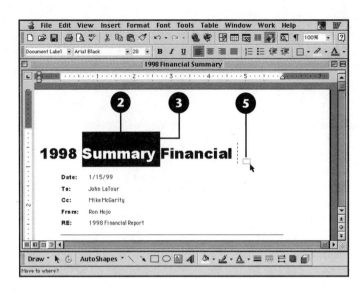

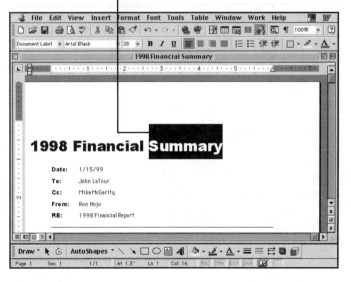

"Summary" dragged from one part of the Word document to another

Finding and Replacing Text

The Find and Replace commands make it easy to search for and, if you want, replace specific text or formulas in a document. The Find And Replace dialog boxes vary slightly from one Office 98 program to the next, but the commands all work essentially the same way.

TIP

Things to remember when you search for text. *When you replace text in Word or PowerPoint, a dialog box will notify you when you have reached the end of the document. When you replace text in Excel, a dialog box will notify you when no more matching data is found.*

Find Text

1. Position the cursor (or insertion point) at the beginning of the document.

2. Click the Edit menu, and then click Find.

3. Type the text you want to locate in the Find What box.

4. Click Find Next until the text you want to locate is highlighted.

5. If a dialog box opens when you reach the end of the document, as it does in some Office programs, click OK.

6. When you're finished, click Close.

You might need to drag the dialog box out of the way to see the highlighted text.

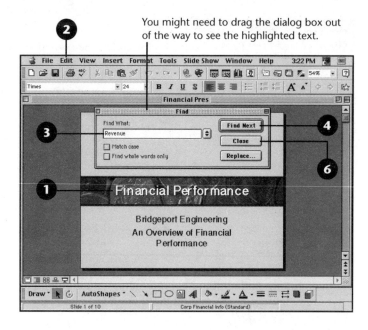

Find and replace special characters and document elements. *In a Word document, you can search for and replace special characters (for example, an em dash) and document elements (for example, a tab character). Click the More button in the Find And Replace dialog box, click Special, and then select the item you want from the pop-up menu.*

Format text you find and replace. *In a Word document, you can search for and replace text with specific formatting features, such as a font and font size. Click the More button in the Find And Replace dialog box, click Format, click the formatting option you want, and then complete the corresponding dialog box.*

Format your company name for greater impact. *Find the name of your company in your latest marketing document that you created in Word. Replace it with a formatted version of the company name (for example, specify a new font and size).*

Replace Text

1 Position the cursor (or insertion point) at the beginning of the document.

2 Click the Edit menu, and then click Replace.

3 Type the text you want to search for in the Find What box.

4 Type the replacement text in the Replace With box.

5 Click Find Next to begin the search and highlight the next instance of the search text.

6 Click Replace to substitute the replacement text and find the next instance of the search text, or click Find Next to locate the next instance of the search text without making a replacement.

7 If a dialog box opens when you reach the end of the document, as it does in some Office programs, click OK.

8 When you're finished, if necessary, click Close.

Changes to Close

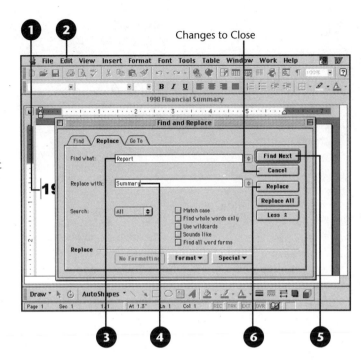

Auto-Correcting Your Text

Since the dawn of typing, people have mistyped certain words or letter combinations consistently. How many times do you misspell "and" or hold down the Shift key too long? *AutoCorrect* corrects common misspellings and incorrect capitalization as you type. It also replaces typed characters, such as -- (two hyphens), with typographical symbols, such as — (an em dash). What's more, you can add your personal problem words to the AutoCorrect list. In most cases, AutoCorrect won't correct errors until you've pressed the Return key or the spacebar.

Replace Text as You Type

◆ To correct incorrect capitalization or spelling errors automatically, continue typing until AutoCorrect makes the required correction.

◆ To replace two hyphens with an em dash, turn ordinals into superscripts (for example, 1st to 1st), or make a fraction stacked (for example, $^{1}/_{2}$) continue typing until AutoCorrect makes the appropriate change.

EXAMPLES OF AUTOCORRECT CHANGES		
Type of Correction	**If You Type**	**AutoCorrect Inserts**
Capitalization	ann marie	Ann Marie
Capitalization	microsoft	Microsoft
Capitalization	thursday	Thursday
Superscript ordinals	2nd	2nd
Stacked fractions	1/2	$^{1}/_{2}$
Em dashes	Madison--a small city in southern Wisconsin--is a nice place to live.	Madison—a small city in southern Wisconsin—is a nice place to live.
Common typos	accomodate	accommodate
Common typos	can;t	can't
Common typos	windoes	windows

Use Undo to change an AutoCorrect change. *To reverse an AutoCorrect change, click the Undo button on the Standard toolbar as soon as AutoCorrect makes the change.*

You can create exceptions to AutoCorrect. *You can also specify abbreviations and terms that you don't want AutoCorrect to automatically correct by clicking the Exceptions button and adding these items to the list of exceptions.*

Customize your AutoCorrect list. *Add your commonly mistyped words to the AutoCorrect list. You can also add abbreviations. Type your initials (in lowercase letters preferably) in the Replace box and your full name in the With box. Then try it: type your initials and press the spacebar, and watch AutoCorrect display your name.*

Add AutoCorrect Entries

1 Click the Tools menu, and then click AutoCorrect.

2 If necessary, click the AutoCorrect tab.

3 In the Replace box, type the incorrect text you want AutoCorrect to correct.

4 In the With box, type the text or symbols you want AutoCorrect to use as a replacement.

5 Click Add.

6 In Word, click any of the tabs to display AutoCorrect formatting settings.

7 When you're finished, click OK.

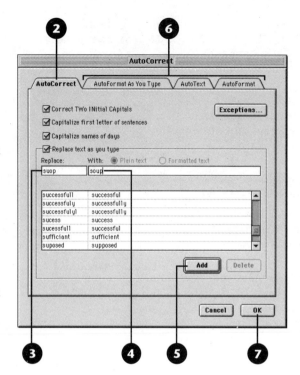

Making Corrections

Everyone makes mistakes and changes their mind at some point, especially when creating or revising a document. With Office 98 you can instantly correct typing errors by pressing a key. You can also reverse more complicated actions, such as typing an entire word, formatting a paragraph, or creating a chart, with the Undo button. If you change your mind, you can just as easily click the Redo button to restore the action you undid.

> **TIP**
>
> **Use undo or redo to reverse or repeat an action.** *To undo or redo a series of actions, continue clicking either the Undo or Redo button until you've reversed or repeated the series of actions.*

> **TIP**
>
> **Use the keyboard to quickly undo your last action.** *Press ⌘+Z. To redo your undo, press ⌘+Y.*

Undo or Redo an Action Using the Standard Toolbar

◆ Click the Undo button to reverse your most recent action, such as typing a word, formatting a paragraph, or creating a chart.

◆ Click the Redo button to restore the last action you reversed.

◆ Click the Undo drop-down arrow, and then click the consecutive actions you want to reverse.

◆ Click the Redo drop-down arrow, and then click the consecutive actions you want to restore.

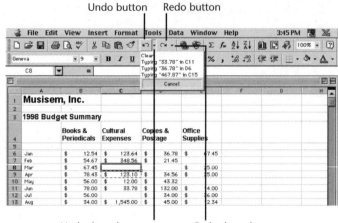

Undo button   Redo button

Undo drop-down arrow   Redo drop-down arrow

CORRECT TYPING ERRORS USING THE KEYBOARD	
To Delete	**Press**
One character at a time to the left of the insertion point	Delete
One word at a time to the left of the insertion point	⌘+Delete
One character at a time to the right of the insertion point	Del
One word at a time to the right of the insertion point	⌘+Del
Selected text	Delete or Del

Reviewing Your Work

When you reveiw an Office 98 document, you can insert your comments right on the document, spreadsheet, or presentation slide. The comments appears in yellow comment boxes (PowerPoint and Excel) or highlighted text (Word). You can move, resize, and reformat the text and the comment boxes just as you can any other object. You can also e-mail your Office 98 document and have others add their comments.

TIP

Hide or display comments quickly. *Click the View menu, and then click Comments.*

SEE ALSO

See "Inserting Comments" on page 110 for information on working with comments in Microsoft Word.

Insert a comment

1 Click in the document where you want to insert a comment.

2 Click the Insert menu, and then click Comment.

3 Type your comments, and then click outside the yellow comments box.

In Excel, a red triangle in the corner of a cell indicates a comment.

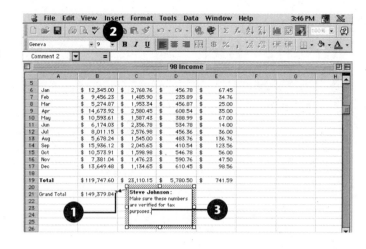

Review Comments Using the Reviewing Toolbar

1 Click the View menu, point to Toolbars, and then click Reviewing.

2 Click the Show/Hide (All) Comments button on the Reviewing toolbar to display comments.

3 Click the Next Comment button or Previous Comment button on the Reviewing toolbar, if available.

Click to e-mail your document

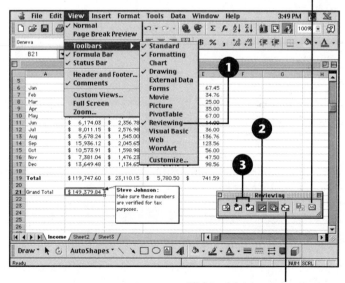

Click to delete a comment

Selecting, Moving, and Resizing Objects

As you learn more about and use each Office 98 product, you will want to enhance your documents with more than just text or numbers. To do so, you can insert an object. An *object* is a picture or a graphic image you create with a drawing program or insert from an existing file of another program. For example, you can insert a company logo that you have drawn yourself, or you can insert a piece of clip art—pictures that come with Office 98. To work with an object, you need to select it first. Once an object is selected, you can resize or move it with its selection *handles*, the little squares that appear on the edge of the object when you click the object to select it.

Select and Deselect an Object

◆ Click an object to display its handles.

◆ Click within the document window to deselect a selected object.

Unselected object
This object has no handles, which means it is not selected.

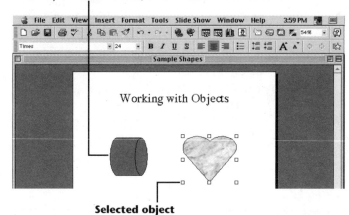

Selected object
Square white handles appear around a selected object.

Move an Object

1. Click an object to select it.

2. Drag the object to a new location as shown by the dotted outline of the object.

3. Release the mouse button to drop the object in the new location.

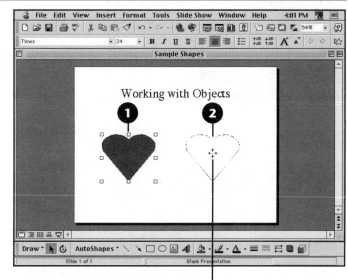

This pointer might look different or not appear at all.

Resize an Object

1. Click the object to be resized.

2. Drag one of the sizing handles:

   ◆ To resize the object in the vertical or horizontal direction, drag a sizing handle on the side of the selection box.

   ◆ To resize the object proportionally in both the vertical and horizontal directions, drag a sizing handle on the corner of the selection box.

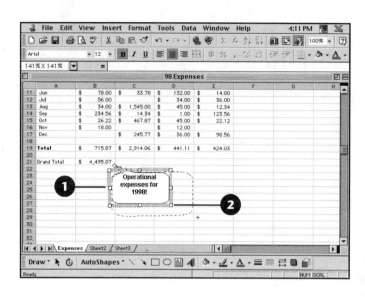

Resize an Object Precisely

1. Click the object to be resized.

2. Click the Format menu, and then click Object, Picture, or AutoShape, depending on the Office program you are using.

3. Click the Size tab.

4. Click the Scale Height and Width spin arrows to resize the object.

5. Click OK.

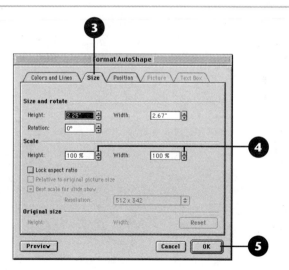

Drawing and Enhancing Objects

Drawn objects, like curved lines or lightning bolts, can liven up your document or help make your point. Using the options on the Drawing toolbar, you can draw numerous objects without leaving the program you happen to be working in. After you add an object to your document, you can improve on it with a host of colors, and special effects that reflect you, your company, or your organization. Simply select the object you want to enhance, and then select the effect you prefer. To make your documents easy to read, take care not to add too many lines, shapes, or other objects.

Draw Lines and Shapes

(1) Click the View menu, point to Toolbars, and then click Drawing.

(2) Click the AutoShapes button on the Drawing toolbar, point to Lines or Basic Shapes, and then select the line or the shape you want.

(3) Click in the document window, drag the pointer until the line or the shape is the size you want, and then release the mouse button.

(4) If you make a mistake, click the Edit menu, and then click Undo, or press the Delete key while the line or shape is still selected and try again.

Click to draw a straight line.

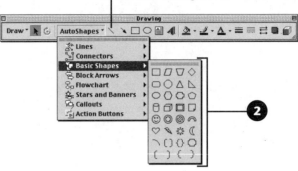

When drawing some curvy lines, you need to click the mouse button once for every curve you want.

Some examples of lines and shapes you can draw using the Drawing toolbar.

Use the Drawing toolbar to align, group, or rotate objects. *Click Draw on the Drawing toolbar to use commands to group, reorder, align or distribute, and rotate or flip objects.*

See "Selecting, Moving, and Resizing Objects" on page 36 for information on working with objects.

Create a design or a logo to add to all your personal correspondence. *Combine colors and shadows or colors and 3-D for the most dramatic effects.*

Add Color, Shadows, and 3-D Effects

Before you can add color, shadows, or 3-D effects to an object, you need to open the Drawing toolbar.

◆ To fill a selected shape with color, click the Fill Color drop-down arrow, and then select the color you want.

◆ To change the line color of a selected object, click the Line Color drop-down arrow, and then select the color you want.

◆ To change the line style of a selected object, click the Line Style button or the Dash Style button, and then select the style you want.

◆ To change the line arrow style of a selected line object, click the Arrow Style button, and then select the style you want.

◆ To add a shadow to a selected object, click the Shadow button, and then select the shadow you want.

◆ To add 3-D to a selected object or text, click the 3-D button, and then select the 3-D effect you want or click 3-D Settings to open the 3-D Settings toolbar.

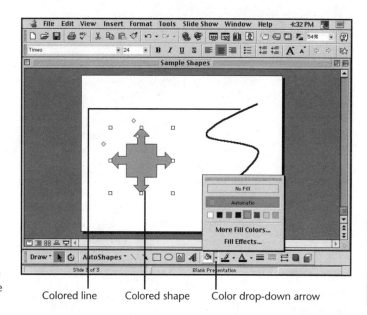

Colored line   Colored shape   Color drop-down arrow

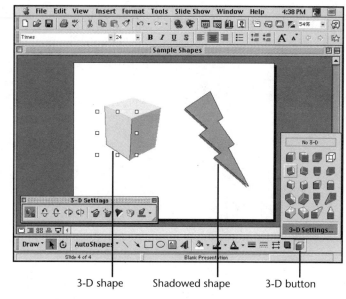

3-D shape   Shadowed shape   3-D button

Adding WordArt

To add life to your documents, you can add a WordArt object to your document. *WordArt* is a Microsoft Office program that allows you to add visual enhancements to your text that go beyond changing a font or a font size. You can select a WordArt style that stretches your text vertically, horizontally, or diagonally. Like many enhancements you can add to a document, WordArt is an object that you can move and reshape.

Insert WordArt button

Create WordArt

(1) Click the Drawing button on the Standard toolbar.

(2) Click the WordArt button on the Drawing toolbar.

(3) Double-click the style of text you want to insert.

(4) Type the text you want in the Edit WordArt Text dialog box.

(5) Click the Font pop-up menu, and then select the font you want.

(6) Click the Size pop-up menu, and then select the font size you want, measured in points.

(7) If you want, click the Bold button, the Italic button, or both.

(8) Click OK.

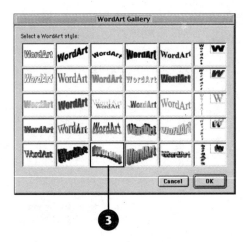

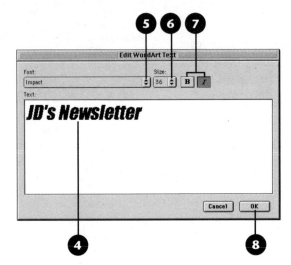

TIP

Use other WordArt toolbar buttons. *Use the WordArt toolbar buttons to rotate your WordArt object, change its alignment, and customize the spacing between each character.*

TIP

Displaying the WordArt toolbar. *When you click a WordArt object, its selection handles and the WordArt toolbar reappear.*

TRY THIS

Create a neighborhood newsletter. *Create a newsletter for your neighborhood's crime-watch group. Use WordArt for the title of the newsletter and some of the article titles.*

TIP

Use the keyboard to delete a WordArt object. *Select the object, and then press Delete.*

⑨ With the WordArt object selected, drag any handle to reshape the object until the text is the size you want.

⑩ Use the WordArt toolbar buttons to format or edit the WordArt object text even more.

⑪ Drag the WordArt object to the location you want.

⑫ Click outside the WordArt object to deselect it and close the toolbar.

USING WORDART TOOLBAR BUTTONS

Icon	Button Name	Description
	Insert WordArt	Create new WordArt
Edit Text...	Edit Text	Edit the existing text in a WordArt object
	WordArt Gallery	Choose a new style for existing WordArt
	Format WordArt	Change the attributes of existing WordArt
Abc	WordArt Shape	Modify the shape of an existing WordArt object
	Free Rotate	Rotate an existing object
Aa	WordArt Same Letter Heights	Make uppercase and lowercase letters the same height
Ab bↀ	WordArt Vertical	Change horizontal letters into a text vertical formation
≡	WordArt Alignment	Change the alignment of an existing object
AV	WordArt Character Spacing	Change the spacing between characters

3

Adding and Modifying Media Clips

You can add pictures, sounds, and videos to Office documents. Your company might have a logo that it includes in all Office documents. Or you might want to use *clip art,* copyright-free graphics, in your document for a special presentation you need to give. A picture is any *graphic object* that you insert as a single unit. You can insert pictures that you've created in a drawing program or scanned in, or you can insert clip art. If you have inserted a picture, you can crop or cut out an image by hand using the Crop tool on the Picture toolbar. To further modify an image, you can change its color to default colors (automatic), grayscale, black and white, or watermark.

Insert Clip Art from the Clip Gallery

1. Select the position where you want to insert a media clip.

2. Click the Insert menu, point to Picture, and then click Clip Art.

3. Click the tab (Clip Art, Pictures, Sounds, or Videos) for the type of clip media you want to insert.

4. Click a category in the list on the left.

5. Click a media clip in the box. If necessary, scroll to see what is available.

6. Click Insert.

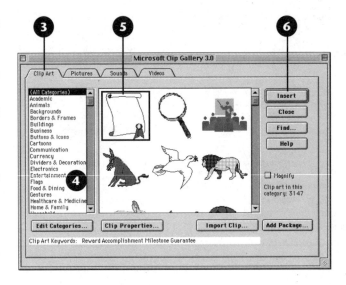

Insert a Picture

1. Click in the document where you want to insert the picture.

2. Click the Insert menu, point to Picture, and then click From File.

3. Open the folder where your picture is stored.

4. Click the image you want to use.

5. Click Insert.

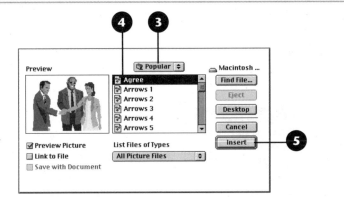

Crop button

TIP

Display the Picture toolbar. *If the Picture toolbar does not appear when you select a picture or clip art, click the View menu , point to Toolbars, and then click Picture.*

TIP

Change a picture's brightness and contrast. *Select a picture, and then click the More Brightness or Less Brightness button on the Picture toolbar, or click the More Contrast or Less Contrast button to the desired effect.*

TIP

Add a border to a picture. *Select a picture, click the Line Style button on the Picture toolbar, and then click the line style you want.*

Crop an Image Quickly

1. Click the image.

2. Click the Crop button on the Picture toolbar.

3. Drag the sizing handles until the borders surround the area you want to crop.

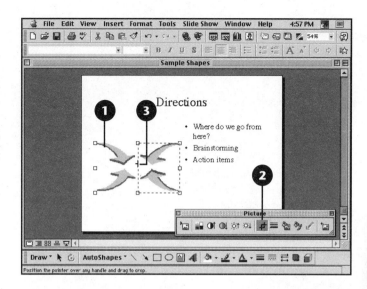

Choose a Color Type

1. Click the object whose color you want to change.

2. Click the Image Control button on the Picture toolbar.

3. Click one of the Image Control options:

   ◆ Automatic (default coloring)

   ◆ Grayscale (whites, blacks, and grays)

   ◆ Black & White (white and black)

   ◆ Watermark (whites and very light colors)

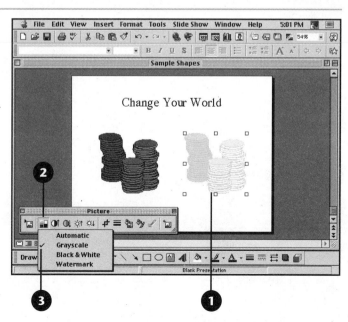

Creating an Organization Chart

An *organization chart* shows the personnel structure in an organization. You can insert an organization chart in an Office 98 document using Microsoft Organization Chart. When you insert an organization chart, chart boxes appear into which you enter company personnel. Each box is identified by its position in the chart. Managers, for example, are at the top, while Subordinates are below, Co-workers to the sides, and so on.

Create a New Organization Chart

1. Click the Insert menu, point to Picture, and then click Organization Chart.

   You can also click the Insert menu, click Object, and then double-click Microsoft Organization Chart 2.0.

2. In the open chart box at the top, type a name.

3. To add a chart box, click a chart box type button on the toolbar, and then click the chart box you want to add a new chart box to.

4. Click in a chart box, select the sample text, and then type a name or text.

5. Click the File menu, and then click Quit And Return.

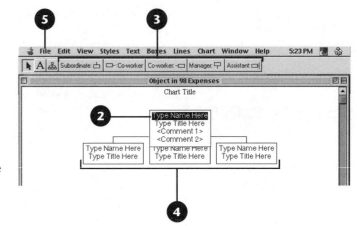

Format an Organization Chart

1. In Organization Chart, click the Edit menu, point to Select, and then click a command to select the chart boxes you want to format.

2. Click the Boxes or Lines menu, point to the area you want to format, and then click the format option you want to choose.

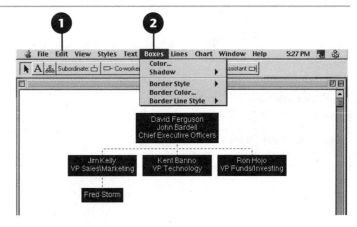

Creating Internet Documents with Office 98

World Wide Web technology is now available for all your Microsoft Office 98 documents. For better productivity and easier compilation of information, you can add *hyperlinks* (graphic or text objects you click to jump to other Office documents and intranet or Internet pages) within your Office documents. (See "Sharing Information Between Programs" on page 220 for more information about embedding hyperlinks in your document).

Once you click several hyperlinks, perhaps opening Word, Excel, and PowerPoint in the process, you also need a way to move between these open documents. The Web toolbar makes this simple with its Web-like navigation tools. You can move backward or forward one document at a time or jump to any document with just a couple of mouse clicks.

In fact, whether a document is stored on your computer, network, intranet, or across the globe, you can access it from Office 98. Just display the Web toolbar from within any Office program, and you're ready to jump to any document, no matter where it resides.

Once you have created a document with hyperlinks, you can save it as an Internet, or HTML, document, and then preview the document using a Web browser, such as Microsoft Internet Explorer.

Inserting Hyperlinks

Sometimes you'll want to refer to another part of the same document or a file created in a different program. Rather than duplicating the material or adding a footnote, you can create a *hyperlink*, a graphic or colored, underlined text object that you click to move (or *jump*) to another location. The jump can be within the same document, to a location in another file on your computer or network, or to a Web page on your intranet or the Internet.

Insert Hyperlink button

Insert a Hyperlink Within a Document

(1) Choose the location from which you want the hyperlink to jump (a Word bookmark, an Excel named range or cell, or a PowerPoint slide number).

(2) Click where you want to insert the hyperlink, type the text you want to use as the hyperlink, and then select it.

(3) Click the Insert Hyperlink button on the Standard toolbar.

(4) Click the Named Location In File Select button, and then double-click the name you want to jump to.

(5) Click OK.

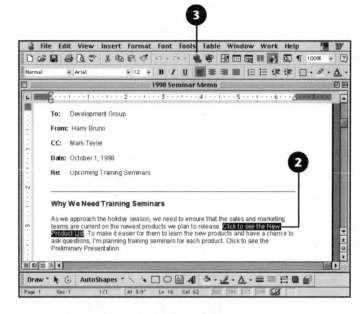

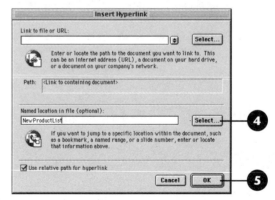

SEE ALSO

See "Jumping to Hyperlinked Documents" on page 52 for information on URLs and Internet addresses.

Insert a Hyperlink Between Documents

(1) Position the insertion point where you want the hyperlink to appear.

(2) Type and then select the text you want to use as the hyperlink.

(3) Click the Insert Hyperlink button on the Standard toolbar.

(4) Click the Link To File Or URL Select button, and then double-click the file you want to jump to.

(5) Click OK.

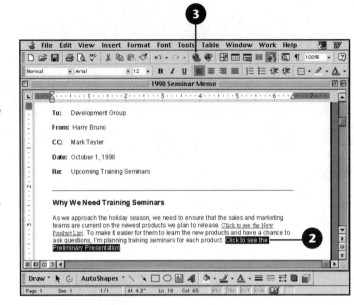

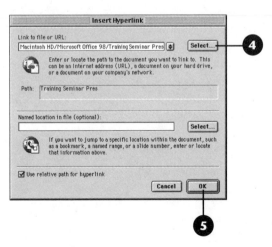

Using and Removing Hyperlinks

Hyperlinks extend a document well beyond that one file. Rather than duplicating the important information stored in other documents, you can create hyperlinks to the relevant material. When you click a hyperlink for the first time (during a session), the color of the hyperlink changes color indicating that you have accessed the hyperlink. If a link becomes outdated or unnecessary, you can easily remove it.

Pointer for clicking
a hyperlink

SEE ALSO

See "Jumping to Hyperlinked Documents" on page 52 for more information about using hyperlinks.

Use a Hyperlink

1. Position the mouse pointer (which changes to a hand cursor) over any hyperlink.

   A ScreenTip appears, displaying the location of the hyperlink.

2. Click the hyperlink. The screen:

   ◆ Jumps to a new location within the same document

   ◆ Jumps to a location on an Intranet or Internet Web site

   ◆ Opens a new file and the program in which it was created

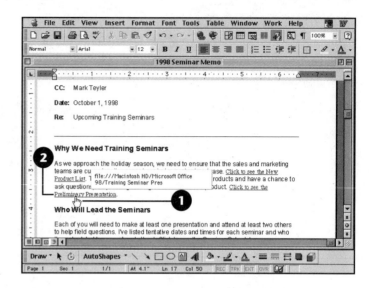

"Hyperlinks make navigating in my reports quick and easy!"

Remove a Hyperlink

(1) Drag the I-beam pointer across the hyperlink to select it without clicking it.

(2) Click the Insert Hyperlink button on the Standard toolbar.

(3) Click Remove Link.

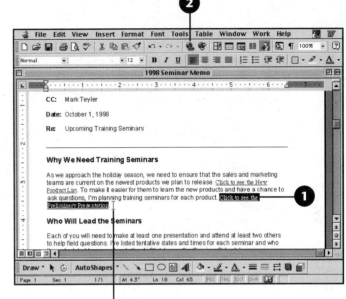

Use this pointer to highlight the hyperlink. If you click the hyperlink, you will jump to another location rather than select it.

Getting Started with the Web Toolbar

The Web toolbar provides an easy way to navigate hyperlinked documents in any Office 98 program. The Web toolbar looks and works the same no matter which Office program you are using. While you're browsing, you can hide all the other toolbars to gain the greatest space available on your screen and improve readability. You can make any document your *start page*, or home base. Set your start page to a document you want to access quickly and frequently.

Web Toolbar button

Display or Hide the Web Toolbar

1 Click the Web Toolbar button on the Standard toolbar. This button toggles on and off to show and hide the Web toolbar.

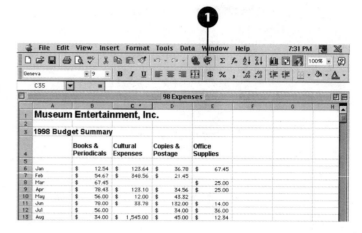

Hide or Display Other Toolbars

1 Click the Show Only Web Toolbar button on the Web toolbar.

Click to make any visible toolbars disappear or reappear.

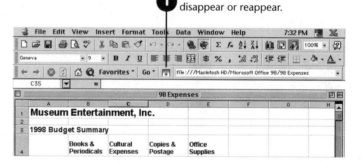

All toolbars are hidden except the Web toolbar.

Start Page button

Jump to Your Start Page

1 Click the Start Page button on the Web toolbar.

TRY THIS

Change your start page. *If you have Internet access, set your start page to the Internet site you visit most frequently or the Web page on your intranet.*

SEE ALSO

See "Getting Information from the Web" on page 56 for information on changing your search page.

Change Your Start Page

1 Open the document you want as your start page.

2 Click the Go button on the Web toolbar.

3 Click Set Start Page.

4 Click Yes to confirm the new start page.

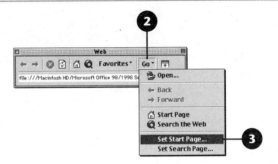

4

Jumping to Hyperlinked Documents

You can jump directly to a document on your computer or network, or to a Web page on your intranet or the Internet using the Web toolbar. In the Address box on the Web toolbar, type the address for the document you want to view and then press Enter. To jump to a document on your hard drive or network, enter its filename including its path (for example, file:///Macintosh HD/Microsoft Office 98/ 1998 Seminar Memo). To jump to a Web document, enter its Internet address (a URL, for example, http://www.microsoft.com).

TIP

Open a Web page in Microsoft Word. *In Word, click the File menu, click Open Web Page, type or select a Web page address, and then click OK.*

Jump to a Document Using the Address Box

(1) Click in the Address box on the Web toolbar to select the current address.

(2) Type an address for the document. For example, file:///Macintosh HD/ Microsoft Office 98/Training Seminar Pres. The address includes:

   ◆ A hard drive (Macintosh HD)

   ◆ One or more folders (Microsoft Office 98)

   ◆ A filename (Training Seminar Pres)

(3) Press Return.

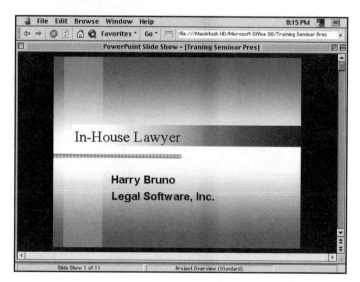

Internet addresses and URLs. *Every Web page has a uniform resource locator (URL), an Internet address in a form your browser program can decipher. Like postal addresses and e-mail addresses, each URL contains specific parts that identify where a Web page is located. For example, the URL for Microsoft's Web page is* ***http://www.microsoft.com/*** *where "http://" shows the address is on the Web and "www.microsoft.com" shows the computer that stores the Web page. As you browse various pages, the URL includes folders and filenames.*

Open a Web document. *In the Address box, enter the complete location of the document you want to open, including the file://folder/ filename. If you have access to the Internet, you can enter a URL for a Web page.*

Jump to a Web Document Using the Address Box

(**1**) Click in the Address box on the Web toolbar to select the current address.

(**2**) Type an Internet address. For example, http:// www.perspection.com (Perspection's Web address).

(**3**) Press Return.

(**4**) Connect to the Internet through your Internet service provider (ISP) or network. Your Web browser opens (such as Microsoft Internet Explorer).

(**5**) Click any hyperlink to explore the Web site.

(**6**) When you are finished, click the File menu, and then click Close.

(**7**) Disconnect from the Internet.

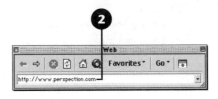

4

Navigating Hyperlinked Documents

As you explore hyperlinked documents, you might want to retrace your steps and return to a document you've already visited. You can move backward and then forward one document at a time, or you can jump directly to any document from the *Address list*, which shows the last 10 documents you've linked to. This way you can quickly jump to any document without having to click through them one by one. After you start the jump to a document, you can stop the link if the document opens (or *loads*) slowly or you decide not to access it. If a document loads incorrectly or you want to update the information it contains, you can reload, or *refresh*, the page.

Back Up One Document

1. Click the Back button on the Web toolbar.

Move Forward One Document

1. Click the Forward button on the Web toolbar until you return to the most recent document you opened.

Jump to Any Open Hyperlinked Document

1. Click the Address drop-down arrow.

2. Click the document or address you want to jump to.

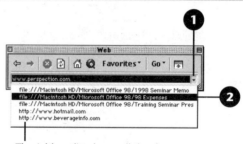

The Address list shows all the documents you've opened this session, in the order you opened them.

Stop Current Jump button

Refresh Current Page button

Stop a Link

(1) Click the Stop Current Jump button on the Web toolbar.

Reload a Document

(1) Click the Refresh Current Page button on the Web toolbar.

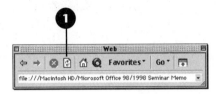

SEE ALSO

See "Inserting Hyperlinks" on page 46 for more information about embedding a link in your Office document to an Internet site or another Office document.

SEE ALSO

See "Using and Removing Hyperlinks" on page 48 for more information about using hyperlinks in Office documents.

4

Getting Information from the Web

You can find all kinds of information on the Web. The best way to find information is to use a search engine. A *search engine* allows you to search through a collection of material to find what you are looking for. There are many search engines available on the Web, such as Yahoo! and Excite. You can make any document your *search page*. Set your search page to a reliable search engine you want to access frequently.

Search The Web button

Search for Information on the Web

(1) Click the Search The Web button on the Web toolbar.

(2) Connect to the Internet through your Internet service provider (ISP) or network. Your Web browser opens (such as Microsoft Internet Explorer).

(3) Click the Search tab.

(4) Click the Select Provider pop-up menu, and then select a search engine.

(5) Type in a topic you want to search for on the Internet.

(6) Click the Search button to start the search.

(7) When you are finished, click the File menu, and then click Close.

(8) Disconnect from the Internet.

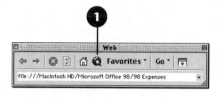

"How can I find information on the Web?"

SEE ALSO

See "Getting Started with the Web Toolbar" on page 51 for information on changing your start page.

Change Your Search Page

(1) Open the document you want as your search page.

(2) Click the Go button on the Web toolbar.

(3) Click Set Search Page.

(4) Click Yes to confirm the new search page.

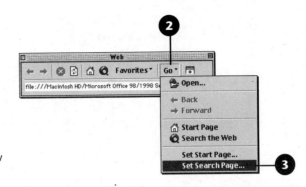

Returning to Favorite Documents

When you have jumped to a document that you would like to return to in the future, you can add the document to a list of favorites. The Favorites button provides shortcuts to files you explore frequently so you won't need to retype long file locations. These shortcuts can open documents on your computer, network, intranet, and the Internet.

TIP

Delete a favorite. *Display the Web toolbar, click the Favorites button, click Open Favorites, select the favorite icon you want to delete, and then press Delete.*

TIP

Edit a favorite. *Display the Web toolbar, click the Favorites button, click Open Favorites, select the favorite text you want to edit, and then modify the text.*

Add a File to Your Favorites List

1. Open the file (or Internet address) you want to access from the Favorites folder.

2. Click the Favorites button on the Web toolbar.

3. Click Add To Favorites.

   Click the Favorites button on the Web toolbar to see the favorite on the menu.

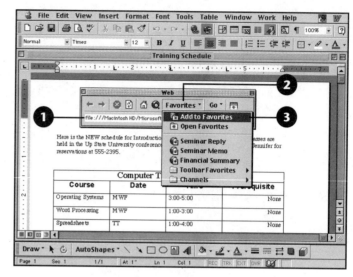

Jump to a Favorite

1. Click the Favorites button on the Web toolbar.

2. Click the favorite document you want to jump to.

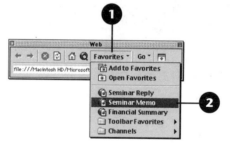

Creating Documents for the Web

You can use the Web Page Wizard in Microsoft Word 98 or the AutoContent Wizard in PowerPoint 98 to create a document or presentation for use on the Web. The Web Page Wizard gives you different layouts and color themes to choose from, such as personal home page, a table of contents, a survey, or a registration form. The AutoContent Wizard gives you an Internet option to create a presentation for the Web. Once the wizard creates a document or presentation, you change the sample information to meet your needs, and then save it in the HTML format.

SEE ALSO

See "Saving Documents for the Web" on page 60 for information on saving a document in the HTML format.

Create a Document for the Web

1. Click the File menu, and then click New.

2. Click the Web Page tab, and then double-click the Web Page Wizard.

3. Select the type of Web page you want to create, and then click Next.

4. Select the visual style you want to create, and then click Finish.

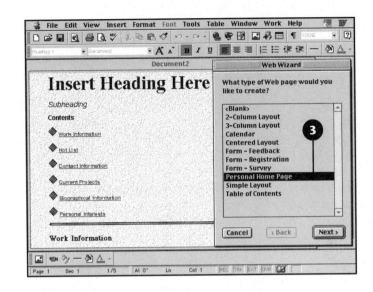

Create a Presentation for the Web

1. Click the File menu, and then click New.

2. Click the General tab, and then double-click AutoContent Wizard.

3. Click Next, select the type of presentation you want to give, and then click Next.

4. Click the Internet, Kiosk option button, and then click Next.

5. Enter an e-mail address and related information, and then click Finish.

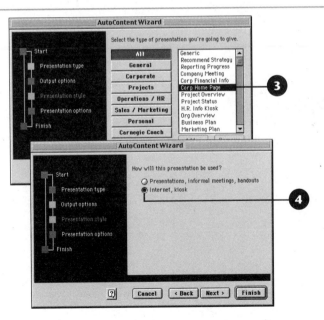

Saving Documents for the Web

Hypertext Markup Language (HTML) is a simple coding system used to format documents for an intranet or the Internet. A browser program interprets these codes to determine how to display a certain document. You can save any open file as an HTML document ready to publish on the World Wide Web or your intranet. When you use the Save As HTML command, it starts the Internet Assistant, which converts your Office document to an HTML document. Then you can publish it on the Web or on your intranet. Be aware that some formatting or other parts of your file might not be available in HTML and therefore might display incorrectly.

Save a Word Document as HTML

1. Open the document you want to save as HTML.
2. Click the File menu, and then click Save As HTML.
3. Select the drive and folder where you want to store the file.
4. Type a name for the file.
5. Click Save and then click Yes to confirm the save.

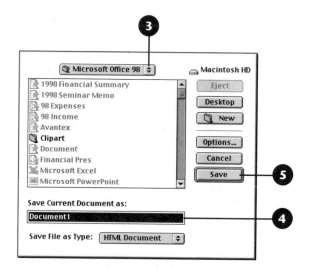

Save an Excel Worksheet as HTML

1. Open the document you want to save as HTML.
2. Click the File menu, and then click Save As HTML.
3. Click Add to specify the ranges and charts to include on the Web page, and then click Next.
4. Click an option buton to create a new Web page or add your data to an existing Web page, and then click Next.
5. Enter header and footer information, and then click Next.

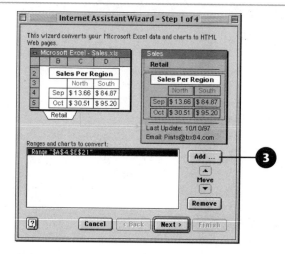

⑥ Type or select the
pathname of the file you
want to save.

⑦ Click Finish.

Internet Assistant Wizard – Step 4 of 4

Type or browse the pathname of the file you want to save.

File path:
Macintosh HD:Microsoft Office 98:MyHTML.html   Select...

Cancel   < Back   Next >   Finish

Save a PowerPoint Presentation as HTML

① Open the document you want to save as HTML.

② Click the File menu, click Save As HTML, and then click Next.

③ Respond to the following tasks one at a time (click Next after each one):

♦ Select a page style (standard or frames).

♦ Select a graphic type (GIF or JPEG).

♦ Select a monitor resolution size.

♦ Enter e-mail and related information.

♦ Select page colors.

♦ Select a button style.

♦ Select a layout option.

♦ Create an HTML folder.

④ Click Finish.

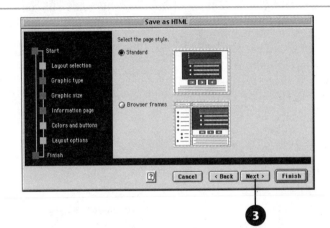

Previewing Web Pages

Once you have created a Web page, or HTML document, you should preview the document in a Web browser, such as Microsoft Internet Explorer, or in Microsoft Word to make sure it looks good when others view the document on the Web. With Internet Explorer, you can preview Web pages on your local hard drive or the Web with ease by entering the Web address in the Address box.

Browse The Internet icon

Preview a Web Page in a Browser

1. Double-click the Internet icon on the desktop.

   Your default Web browser (such as Microsoft Internet Explorer) opens.

2. Click in the Address box on the Address bar.

3. Type an address to the Web page (HTML document) you want to preview.

4. Press Return.

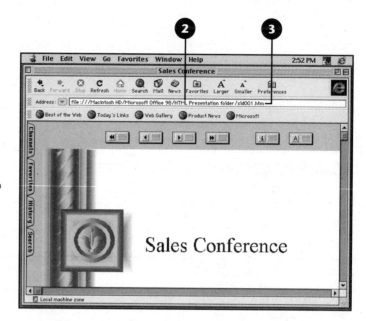

Preview a Web Page in Word

1. Double-click the Microsoft Word icon in the Microsoft Office 98 folder.

2. Click the File menu, and then click Open Web Page.

3. Type or select an address to the Web page (HTML document) you want to preview.

4. Click OK.

Creating a Document with Word 98

Welcome to Microsoft Word 98. This section will familiarize you with this program's many features to help you produce professional-looking documents. You'll learn the most efficient methods to complete the tasks involved in creating documents.

Introducing Word

Microsoft Word, a *word processing program*, is designed to help you create and edit letters, reports, mailing lists, and tables as easily as possible. The files you create and save in Word are known as *documents*. Documents usually include not only text, but also graphics, bulleted lists, and various desktop publishing elements such as drop caps and headlines.

For most people, the real beauty of Word is its editing capabilities. For example, if you don't like where a paragraph is located in a document, you can cut it out and paste it in a new location just by clicking a couple of buttons on the toolbar. Then you can quickly add formatting elements like boldface and special fonts to make your documents look professional and up-to-date.

Viewing the Word Window

Menu bar
The eleven menus give you access to all Word options. Simply click a menu name to display a list of related menu commands, and then click the command you want to issue.

Title bar
The name of the document appears in the title bar. "Document 1" is a temporary name Word uses until you assign a new one.

Standard and Formatting toolbars
These and other toolbars contain buttons that give you quick access to a variety of Word commands and features. If you're not sure what a specific tool does, move the mouse pointer over it to display the name of the toolbar button.

Insertion point
The blinking insertion point (also called a cursor) shows you where the next character you type will appear.

End mark
This short horizontal line indicates the end of the document.

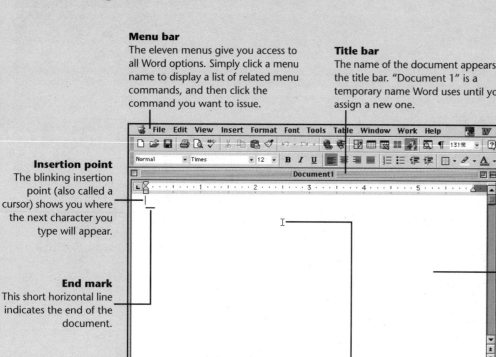

Document window
You enter text and graphics here. As with all Macintoch applications, the document window can be maximized or minimized to best suit your needs.

Status bar
The status bar tells you the location of the insertion point in a document and provides information about the current settings and commands.

Document view buttons
Click to see your document in different ways. Normal view is best for typing and editing. Online layout view shows your document as it will appear on the World Wide Web. Switch to page layout view to see how the printed page will look. Use outline view to create a document outline.

Mouse pointer
In a document window, the mouse pointer appears as an I-beam. The pointer shape changes depending on where you point in the Word document.

Changing Document Views

Normal view

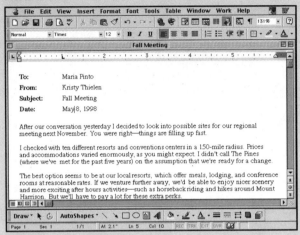

Page Layout view

Online Layout view

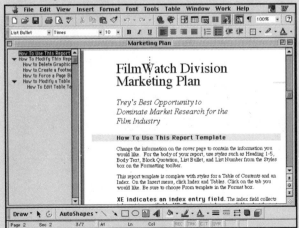

Outline view

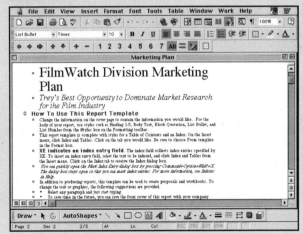

5

Creating a Document

After starting Word, you'll see a new blank document in the document window, ready for you to begin entering text. You can open and work on as many new documents as you'd like. As you type text, Word moves, or *wraps*, the insertion point to a new line when the previous one is full. You can move the insertion point anywhere within the document either by clicking in the desired location or by pressing an arrow key.

TIP

Use Word's nonprinting characters to manage document formatting. *To hide them, click the Show/Hide button on the Standard toolbar.*

¶

SEE ALSO

See "Working with Templates" on page 92 for information about creating a new document from a template.

Enter and Delete Text in a Document

1 Click where you want to insert or delete text.

2 Begin typing.

3 Press Return when you want to begin a new paragraph or insert a blank line.

4 Press Delete to delete text to the left of the insertion point, or press Del to delete text to the right of the insertion point.

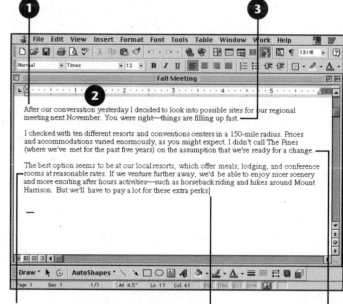

Characters automatically wrap to the next line within a paragraph.

The characters you type appear at the location of the insertion point.

Press Return to begin a new paragraph.

Open a New Document

1 Click the New button on the Standard toolbar.

A blank new document window opens.

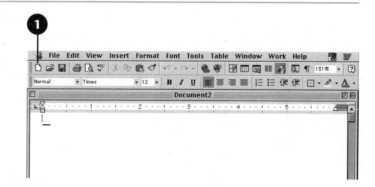

Moving Around in a Document

As your document gets longer, some of your work will shift out of sight. You can easily move any part of a document back into view by *scrolling, paging,* or *browsing.* Sometimes you'll want to switch views for easier editing and to see how your printed document will look. In all four document views, you can use the tools described here to move around your document.

SEE ALSO

See "Finding and Replacing Text and Formatting" on page 74 for information about locating specific text and formatting.

Scroll, Page, and Browse Through a Document

◆ To scroll through the document one line at a time, click the up or down scroll arrow on the vertical scroll bar.

◆ To scroll quickly through an entire document, click and hold the up or down scroll arrow on the vertical scroll bar.

◆ To scroll to a specific page in the document, click and drag the scroll box on the vertical scroll bar until the page number you want appears in the yellow box.

To page through the document one page at a time, press Page Up or Page Down on the keyboard.

◆ To browse by page, edits, headings, or other items, click the Browse button and then click the item you want to browse by. If a dialog box opens, enter the page or item you want to find, and then click the Up and Down Browse Arrow buttons to move from one item to the next.

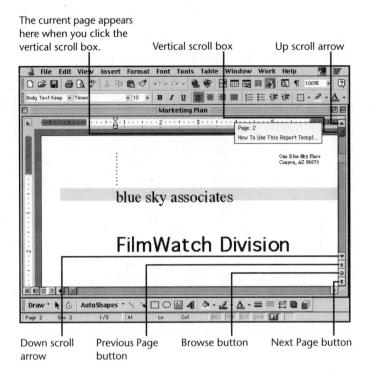

The current page appears here when you click the vertical scroll box.

Vertical scroll box

Up scroll arrow

Down scroll arrow

Previous Page button

Browse button

Next Page button

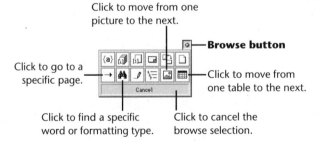

Click to move from one picture to the next.

Browse button

Click to go to a specific page.

Click to move from one table to the next.

Click to find a specific word or formatting type.

Click to cancel the browse selection.

Working with Multiple Documents

The only difference between working with one open document and working with multiple open documents is that you need to make a document active before you can edit it. The same is true when you view different parts of the same document in two windows simultaneously. No matter how you display a document or documents, Word's commands and toolbar buttons work the same as usual.

Switch Between Open Documents

1 Click the Window menu.

2 Click the document you want to work on next.

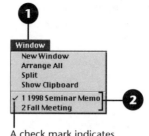

A check mark indicates which document is active.

View All Open Documents Simultaneously

1 Click the Window menu, and then click Arrange All.

◆ Each document has its own title bar, ruler, and vertical scroll bar.

2 Click in the window of the document you want to work on (becomes the active document), and then edit the document as usual.

3 To display only one document again, click the Zoom box in the active document window.

The title bar of the inactive document is grayed out.

Inactive document

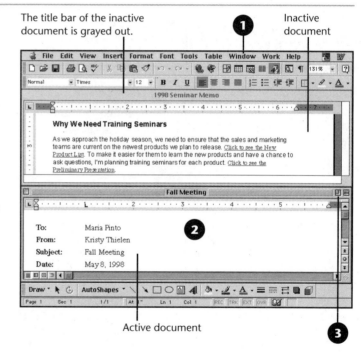

Active document

Work on Two Parts of the Same Document

1 Click the Window menu, and then click Split.

2 Drag the split bar until the two window panes are the sizes you want.

3 Click in the document window to set the split and display a vertical scroll bar and rulers for each pane.

4 Click in each pane and scroll to the parts of the document you want to work on. Each pane scrolls independently.

5 Click in the pane you want to work in, and edit the text as usual.

6 To return to a single pane, click the Window menu, and then click Remove Split.

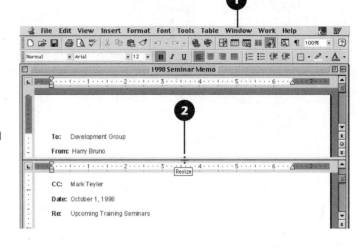

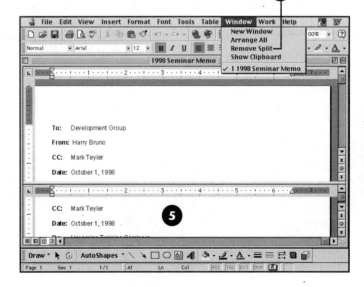

Setting Up the Page

Every document you produce and print might need a different look. To specify how the printed page appears, use the Page Setup dialog box, which, among other things, allows you to specify paper size and *Portrait* (vertical) or *Landscape* (horizontal) orientation. After making any change, you should preview the document before you print.

SEE ALSO

See "Printing a Document" on page 80 for information on printing and printing options.

TIP

Change document margins. *Open the Page Setup dialog box, click the pop-up menu, select Microsoft Word, click Margins, and then makes the necessary changes.*

Set Up the Page

1. Click the File menu, and then click Page Setup.

2. If necessary, click the Format For pop-up menu, and then select the size of the paper in your printer.

3. If necessary, click the Paper pop-up menu, and then select the printer you are using.

4. If necessary, change the page orientation.

5. Click the Page Setup pop-up menu, and then select Microsoft Word.

6. Click the Apply Size And Orientation To pop-up menu, and then select This Section, This Point Forward, or Whole Document.

7. To customize the paper size, click Custom, enter a width and height size, and then click OK.

8. To make your changes the default settings for all new documents, click Default and then click Yes.

9. Click OK.

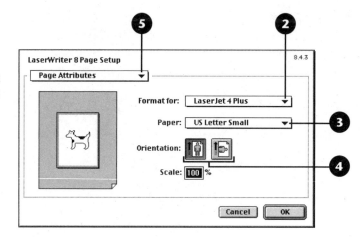

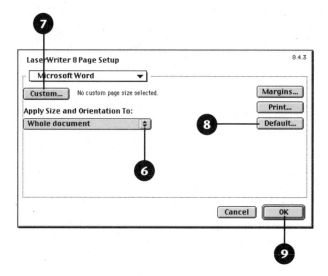

Selecting Text

The first step in working with text is to highlight, or *select*, the text you want to work with. Once you've selected it, you can copy, move, format, and delete words, sentences, and paragraphs. You can even align text easily by first selecting the text you want to adjust. If you finish with or decide not to use a selection, you can click anywhere in the document to *deselect* it.

TIP

Use Undo to restore deleted text. *If, after you select text, you accidentally press Return and delete the text by mistake, click the Undo button on the Standard toolbar to reverse your action.*

SEE ALSO

See "Moving and Copying Text" on page 72, "Formatting Text for Emphasis" on page 82, and "Editing Your Text" on page 28 for more information on the various tasks you can perform with selected text.

Select Text

(1) Position the pointer in the word, paragraph, line, or part of the document you want to select.

(2) Choose a method to select the text you want. Refer to the table for methods to select text.

SELECTING TEXT

To Select	Do This
A single word	Double-click the word.
A single paragraph	Triple-click a word within the paragraph.
A single line	Click in the left margin next to the line.
Any part of a document	Click at the beginning of the text you want to highlight, and then drag to the end of the section you want to highlight.
The entire document	Triple-click in the left margin.

(2) Black highlighting indicates this text is selected.

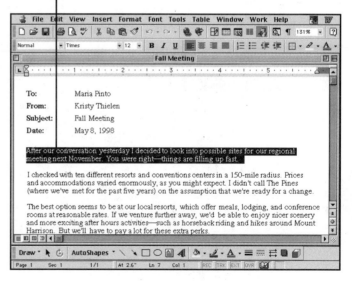

5

Moving and Copying Text

You can move selected text by cutting and then pasting it in a new location. Or you can copy it and then paste the copy in a different location. You can paste multiple copies of text into your document from the *Clipboard*, a temporary storage area that holds your copies until they are replaced by new cut or copied text.

TIP

Go to a specific location.
If you want to move or copy selected text in a location that isn't on your screen, press F5 to display the Go To tab in the Find And Replace dialog box, and then specify the page, section, bookmark, comment, or other location you want to go to.

Move or Copy Using the Standard Toolbar

1. Select the text you want to move or copy.
2. Click the Cut or Copy button on the Standard toolbar.
3. Click in the new location.
4. Click the Paste button on the Standard toolbar.

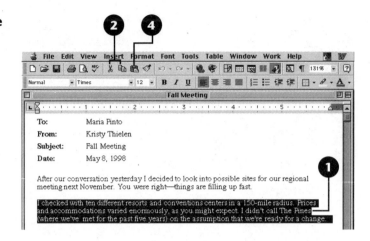

Move or Copy Text by Dragging It

1. Select the text you want to move or copy.
2. Move the pointer over the selected text.
3. To move the text to a new location, click and hold the mouse button.

   To copy the text to a new location, also press and hold the Option key.

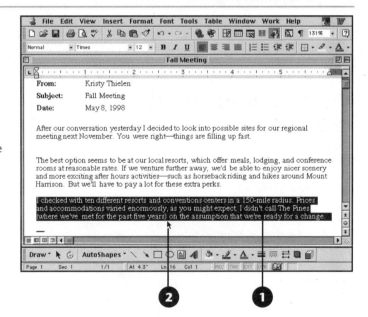

(4) Drag the mouse pointer to the new location, and release the button (and the Option key, if necessary).

(5) Click anywhere in the document to deselect the text.

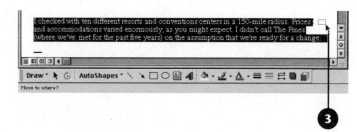

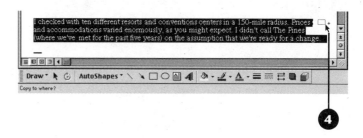

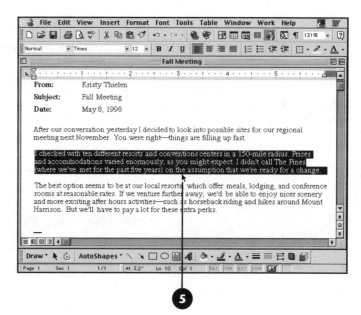

Finding and Replacing Text and Formatting

The Find command makes it easy to locate specific text and formatting in a long document. You can use the Replace command to substitute different text and formatting instantly. The Find And Replace dialog box provides many options that help you find and replace exactly what you want. To fine-tune a search, the Match Case option will enable you to find words that begin with an uppercase letter or that are set in all lowercase or uppercase letters. You can even use a wildcard to find series of words. For example, the search text "ran*" will find "ranch," "ranger," rank," "ransom," and so on. The Go To tab helps you move quickly to a specific location in your document.

Find Text and Formatting

1. Click the Edit menu, and then click Find.

2. Type the text you want to locate in the Find What box.

3. Click the More button, and then select the formatting and search options you want to use.

4. Click Find Next repeatedly to locate each instance of the specified criteria.

5. When you see a message that Word has finished searching the document, click OK.

6. Click Cancel.

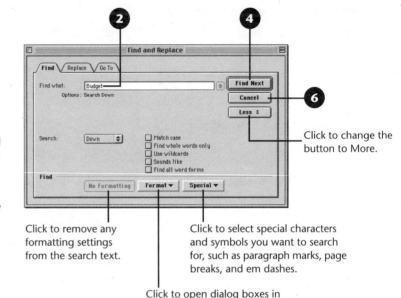

Click to change the button to More.

Click to remove any formatting settings from the search text.

Click to open dialog boxes in which you can specify formatting you want to locate.

Click to select special characters and symbols you want to search for, such as paragraph marks, page breaks, and em dashes.

Find Information by Type

1. Click the Edit menu, and then click Go To.

2. Click the type of location or information you want to move to.

3. Enter the item number (or bookmark name).

4. Click Go To and then Next or Previous, if necessary.

5. Click Close.

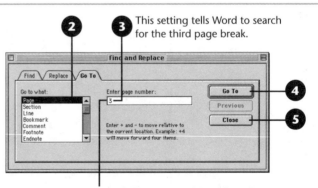

This setting tells Word to search for the third page break.

To find all instances of the selected item, leave the Enter box empty.

Replace Text and Formatting

1 Click the Edit menu, and then click Replace.

2 Type the text you want to locate in the Find What box.

3 Click the More button. and then select the formatting you want to locate, if any, and the search options you want to use (optional).

4 Type the text you want to substitute in the Replace With box.

5 Select the formatting, if any, you want to substitute.

6 Click the Find Next, Replace, or Replace All button.

7 When you see a message that Word has finished searching the document, click OK.

8 Click Cancel.

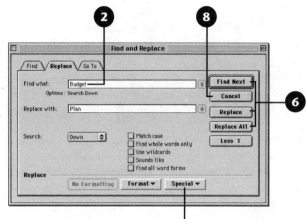

Click to select special characters and symbols you want to locate or to use to replace search text.

5

Checking Your Spelling and Grammar

As you type, Word inserts a wavy red line under words it can't find in its dictionary (such as misspellings or names) or duplicated words (for example, the the). You can correct these errors as they arise or after you finish the entire document. Before you print your final document, it's a good idea to check for grammatical errors using the spelling and grammar checker.

TIP

Use AutoCorrect to correct spelling as you type.
Control-click a commonly misspelled word, point to AutoCorrect, and then click the correct spelling. Auto-Correct automatically corrects the misspelling as you type.

SEE ALSO

See "AutoCorrecting Your Text" on page 32 for more information on correcting misspelled words as you type.

Correct a Misspelled Word as You Type

1 Control-click any word with a red wavy underline to display the Spelling shortcut menu.

2 Click a suggested substitution, tell Word to ignore all instances of the word, or add the word to your dictionary.

If you have a lot of spelling errors, it's easier to use the Spelling And Grammar Checker to find and correct them.

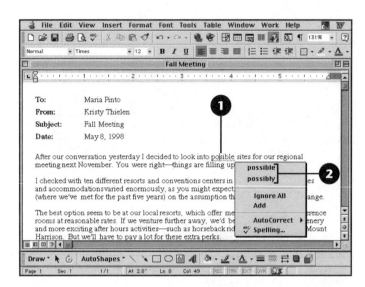

Change Spelling and Grammar Preferences

1 Click the Tools menu, and then click Preferences.

2 Click the Spelling & Grammar tab.

3 Click the check boxes to select or deselect Spelling options.

4 Click the check boxes to select or deselect Grammar options.

5 Click OK.

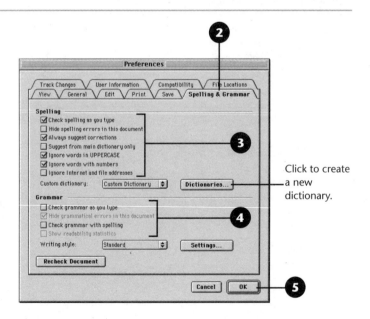

Click to create a new dictionary.

Spelling And Grammar button

TIP

Select text to check a specific part of a document. *You can check spelling, grammar, or usage in part of a document by first selecting the text you want to check. Then follow the steps for checking the entire document.*

TIP

Check just spelling. *If you want to just check your spelling, clear the Check Grammar check box in the Spelling And Grammar dialog box.*

TRY THIS

Add your name to the dictionary. *Add your own first and last name to Word's dictionary so your name will never be flagged as a misspelling.*

Correct Spelling and Grammar

1 Click at the beginning of the document, and then click the Spelling And Grammar button on the Standard toolbar.

2 As it checks each sentence in the document, Word highlights misspelled words in the Not In Dictionary box or problematic sentences in the Sentence box, and displays an appropriate alternative in the Suggestions box.

3 To make a substitution, select any of the suggestions, and then click Change.

4 To skip the word or rule, click Ignore, or to skip every instance of the word or rule, or click Ignore All.

5 If none of Word's suggestions seem appropriate, click in the document and edit it yourself. Click the Resume button to continue.

6 When the grammar check is complete, Word displays a list of readability statistics. Click OK to return to the document.

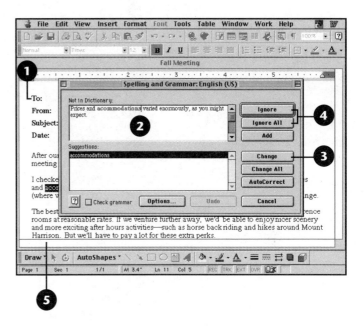

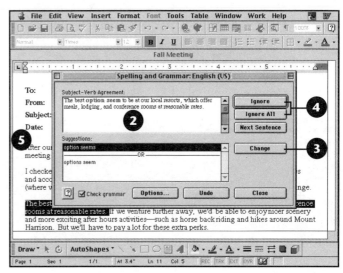

5

Checking Your Word Usage

Using the same word over and over in a document can sometimes take away from your message's effectiveness. If you need help finding exactly the right word, check Word's Thesaurus. Using this feature can save you time and improve the quality and level of readability of your document.

SEE ALSO

See "Checking Your Spelling and Grammar" on page 76 for information on checking spelling.

TIP

Add hyphenation to your document. *Hyphenation eliminates gaps (of white space) in your documents. Click the Tools menu, point to Language, click Hyphenation, and then select the options you want to use.*

Use the Thesaurus

1. Select or type the word in the document you want to look up.

2. Click the Tools menu, point to Language, and then click Thesaurus.

3. Click a word in the Meanings box to display its synonyms in the Replace With Synonym box.

4. If you want to see more choices or words with opposite meanings, click Related Words or Antonyms in the Meanings box. (These options are not available for every word.)

5. If you want to continue looking up synonyms, click a word in the Replace With box for which you want to find synonyms, antonyms, or related words, and then click Look Up.

6. When you find the word you want to use, click it, and then click Replace.

7. If you can't find a replacement word, click Cancel.

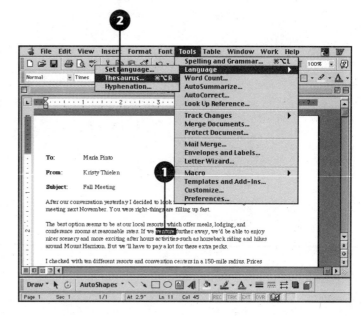

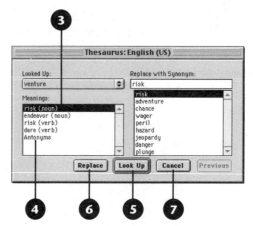

Previewing a Document

If you preview your document before you print, you will save yourself time and money. *Print Preview* shows you exactly how your text will fit on each printed page. This is especially helpful when you have a multiple page document divided into sections with different headers and footers for each section. The Print Preview toolbar provides the tools you need to better analyze how the text is presented on each page.

Print Preview button

SEE ALSO

See "Setting Margins" on page 90 for information on adjusting the space between the edge of a page and the text in a header or footer.

Preview a Document

(1) Click the Print Preview button on the Standard toolbar.

◆ View one page

   Click the One Page button 🔲 to view one page at a time.

◆ View multiple pages

   Click the Multiple Pages button ⊞ to view more than one page at a time.

◆ Change view size

   Click the Zoom drop-down arrow to select a screen display magnification.

◆ Shrink to fit page

   Click the Shrink To Fit button 🔲 to shrink the document by one page.

◆ Display full screen

   Click the Full Screen button 🔲 to display the document with only the toolbar visible.

(2) When you're done, click the Close button on the Print Preview toolbar.

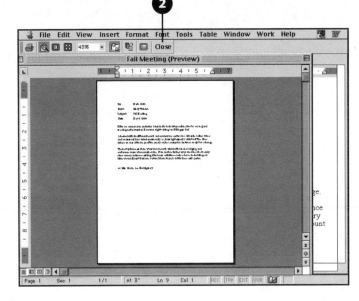

5

Printing a Document

Printing is one of the most essential tasks you need to master. Word makes printing easy, and its options give you the flexibility to print your document just as you want it. The Print button on the Standard toolbar prints one copy of your document using the current settings. If you need more options, use the Print command on the File menu. You can select any printer that is available to you. The Print What option lets you print more than just your document. You can choose to print your annotations, a list of styles used in the document, and AutoText entries, just to name a few. You can specify specific pages to print, as well as the number of copies you want to print.

Print button

Print a Document Quickly

1 Click the Print button on either the Standard toolbar or the Print Preview toolbar.

One copy of your document using the current settings is printed.

Print a Page with Options

1 Click the File menu, and then click Print.

2 Click the Printer pop-up menu and then select the printer you want.

3 Type the number of copies you want to print.

4 Specify the pages you want to print.

5 Specify the paper source you want to use.

6 Click the pop-up menu, and then select Microsoft Word to set other options.

7 Click Word Options to specify Word printing preferences (optional).

8 Click Print.

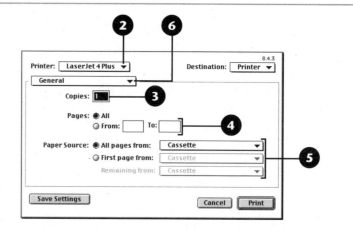

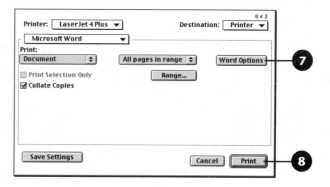

Formatting a Document with Word 98

6

As you become more comfortable with Microsoft Word 98, you will want to use its extensive word processing and desktop publishing features to format the information in your documents. To make sure the document looks professional, you will set tabs, create indents, adjust line and paragraph spacing, and format text for emphasis with italics, boldface, and underline, just to name a few. You might also want to know how to create bulleted and numbered lists, or, perhaps, how to create a form letter in four simple steps. Each and every one of these tasks is made easy with Word.

Templates and Styles

Word documents are based on *templates*, which are predesigned and preformatted files that serve as the basis of a variety of Word documents, such as memos, reports, and cover pages for faxes. Each template is made up of *styles*, which have common design elements, such as fonts and sizes, colors, and page layout designs. A template can have styles for headings, bulleted and numbered lists, body text, and headers and footers. You can also modify a template or style, or create one of your own to better suit your needs.

Formatting Text for Emphasis

You'll often want to *format*, or change the style, of certain words or phrases to add emphasis to parts of a document. **Bold**, *italics*, <u>underlines</u>, highlights, and other text effects are *toggle switches*, which means you simply click to turn them on and off. For special emphasis you can combine formats, such as bold and italics. Using one *font*, or letter design, for headings and another for main text adds a professional look to your document.

TRY THIS

Color your text. *Try brightening up a document by using the Color box in the Font dialog box to change selected text to a color of your choice. Of course, unless you have a color printer, colored text (as well as highlighting) will print in shades of gray.*

Format Existing Text Quickly

1 Select the text you want to emphasize.

2 Click the Bold, Italic, Underline, or Highlight button on the Formatting toolbar.

◆ Remember that you can add more than one formatting option at a time. For example, this text uses both boldface and italics.

3 Click anywhere in the document to deselect the formatted text.

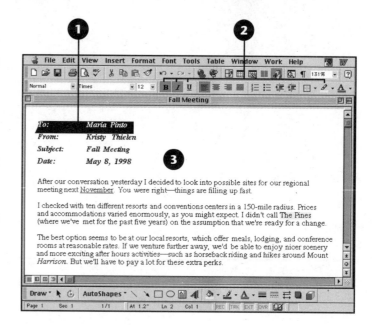

Change the Font or Size of Existing Text Quickly

1 Select the text you want to format.

2 Click the Font menu or click the Font drop-down arrow on the Formatting toolbar, and then select a new font.

3 Click the Font Size drop-down arrow on the Formatting toolbar, and then select a new point size.

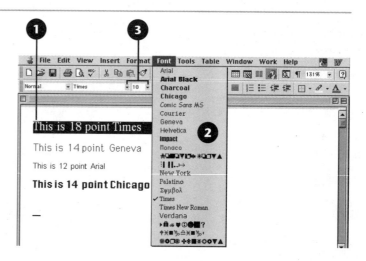

TIP

Format text as you type.
You can add most formatting options to text as you type. First select the formatting options or changes you want, and then type the text. If necessary, turn off the formatting options when you're done.

TRY THIS

Highlight key points in a memo. *Open an existing memo, and then use the Highlight button to highlight key points in your memo with a bright yellow color.*

SEE ALSO

See "Creating and Modifying a Style" on page 96 for information about using Word styles to format text consistently throughout a document.

Apply Formatting Effects to Text

(1) Select the text you want to format.

(2) Click the Format menu, and then click Font.

(3) Click the Font tab.

♦ To change character spacing settings, click the Character Spacing tab.

♦ To add animation effects, click the Animation tab.

(4) Select the formatting options you want to apply.

(5) In the Effects area, click the options you want.

(6) Check the results in the Preview box.

(7) Click OK.

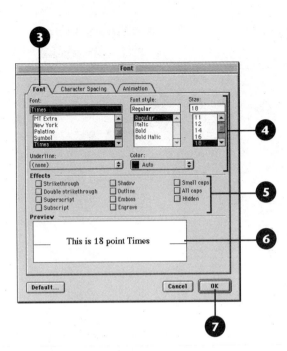

Setting Text Alignment

Word documents by default are aligned on the left, with the text uneven, or *ragged*, on the right margin. Left-aligned text works well for most documents, but you can easily change the alignment of selected paragraphs. *Right-aligned text*, which lines up smoothly along the right margin and is ragged along the left margin, is good for adding a date to a letter. *Justified text* spreads out evenly between the two margins, creating a clean, professional look. *Centered text*, useful for titles and headings, places the text in the middle between the margins.

TIP

Set text alignment before you type. *You can also set the text alignment before you type. Just click the appropriate alignment button on the Formatting toolbar, and then type the text you want.*

Left or Right Align Text

1 Click anywhere in the paragraph or select multiple paragraphs you want to align.

2 Click the Align Left or Align Right button on the Formatting toolbar.

Left-aligned text

Right-aligned text

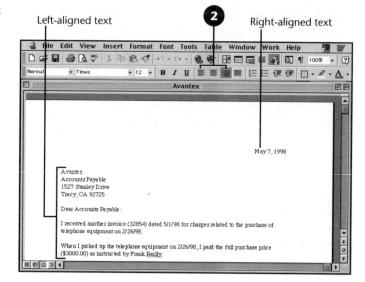

Center or Justify Text

1 Click anywhere in the paragraph or select multiple paragraphs you want to align.

2 Click the Center or Justify button on the Formatting toolbar.

Centered text

Justified text

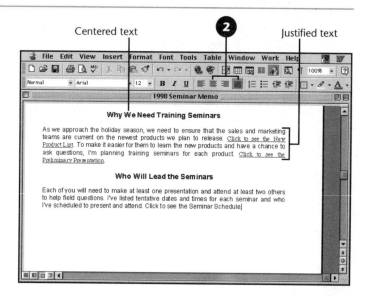

Setting Line Spacing

The lines in all Word documents are single-spaced by default, which is appropriate for letters and most documents. But you can easily change your document to double or one-and-half-spaced lines to allow extra space between every line. This is useful when you want to make notes on a printed document. Sometimes, you'll want to add space above and below certain paragraphs, such as for headlines or indented quotations to help set off the text.

Change Line Spacing

1. Select the paragraph or paragraphs that you want to change.

2. Click the Format menu, click Paragraph, and then click the Indents And Spacing tab.

3. Click the Line Spacing pop-up menu, and then select the option you want.

4. If necessary, type the precise line spacing you want in the At box.

5. Click OK.

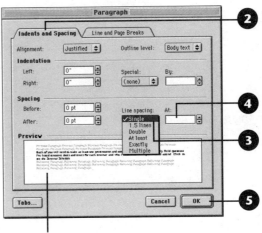

Preview your selections.

Change Paragraph Spacing

1. Select the paragraph you want to change.

2. Click the Format menu, click Paragraph, and then click the Indents And Spacing tab.

3. To add space above a selected paragraph, click the Before up or down arrow.

4. To add space below each selected paragraph, click the After up or down arrow.

5. Click OK.

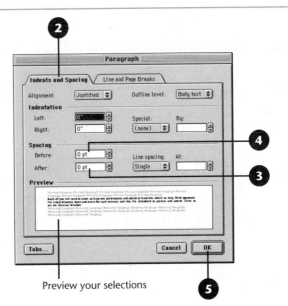

Preview your selections

6

Displaying Rulers

There are two rulers that appear in the Word document window: the horizontal ruler and the vertical ruler. The *horizontal ruler* appears across the top of the document window and shows the length of the typing line. You use the horizontal ruler to adjust margins and indents quickly, set tabs, and adjust column widths. The *vertical ruler* appears along the left edge of the document window and allows you to adjust top and bottom margins of the document page and the row height in tables. Word automatically displays the horizontal ruler in normal view, and both rulers in page layout view; however, you can choose to hide the rulers if you want.

Show and Hide the Rulers

1. Click the View menu, and then click Ruler.

   ◆ To display the horizontal ruler, click the Normal View button.

   ◆ To display both rulers, click the Page Layout View button.

①

Normal view shows only the horizontal ruler.

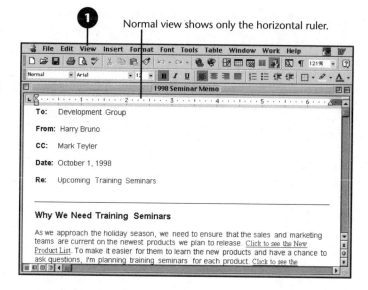

Page Layout view shows both the horizontal and the vertical ruler.

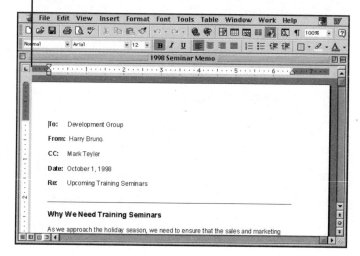

Setting Paragraph Tabs

You can use tabs in your document to adjust how text or numerical data aligns in relation to the document margins. A *tab stop* is a predefined stopping position along the document's typing line. Word's default tab stops are set every half inch, and you can set more than one tab per paragraph. There are four tab stops you can use to align your text: left, right, center, and decimal (for numerical data).

Create and Clear a Tab Stop

1 Select the paragraph(s) for which you want to set a tab stop.

2 Click the Tab button on the horizontal ruler until it shows the type of tab stop you want.

3 Click on the ruler where you want to set the tab stop.

4 If necessary, drag the tab stop to position it exactly where you want.

5 To clear a tab stop, drag it off the ruler.

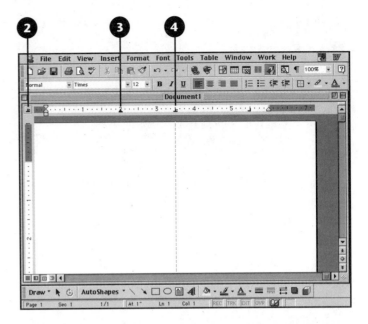

USING THE KEYBOARD FOR LAYOUT	
Tab Stop	**Purpose**
L	Aligns text to the left of the tab stop
⅃	Aligns text to the right of the tab stop
⊥	Centers text on the tab stop
⊥	Aligns numbers on the decimal point

Setting Paragraph Indents

The horizontal ruler makes it easy to indent entire paragraphs from the right or left margin. You can indent just the first line or just the second and subsequent lines of a paragraph from the left margin. You can also use the Increase and Decrease Indent buttons on the Formatting toolbar. If you prefer to use the Indent buttons, keep in mind that they indent text according to Word's default tab stops, which occur every half inch across the width of the document.

TIP

Use the Tab key to quickly indent a line. *You can quickly indent the first line of a paragraph by pressing the Tab key.*

SEE ALSO

See "Creating Bulleted and Numbered Lists" on page 98 for information on aligning and indenting text using lists.

Indent a Paragraph Using the Ruler

Position the insert pointer in the paragraph you want to indent. Use one of the following indent markers on the ruler:

◆ To change the left indent of the first line of text, drag the First-Line Indent marker at the top of the ruler.

◆ To change the indent of the second line of text, drag the Hanging Indent marker.

◆ To change the left indent for all lines of text, drag the Left Indent marker.

◆ To change the right indent for all lines of text, drag the Right-Indent marker.

As you drag an indent marker, a dotted guideline appears on the screen to help you position the indent accurately.

Indent a Paragraph Using the Toolbar

Position the insert pointer in the paragraph you want to indent. Use one of the following Formatting toolbar buttons:

◆ To move the entire paragraph to the right, click the Increase Indent button.

◆ To move the entire paragraph to the left, click the Decrease Indent button.

First-Line Indent marker   Right-Indent marker

Hanging Indent marker   Left Indent marker

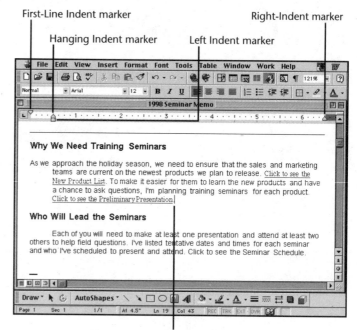

The current indent settings appear on the ruler for this paragraph.

Decrease Indent button   Increase Indent button

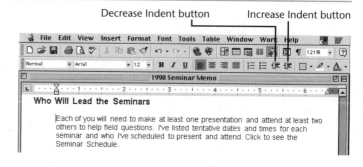

Increase Indent button

Decrease Indent button

SEE ALSO

See "Displaying Rulers" on page 86 for information about displaying and hiding the horizontal ruler.

TIP

Use the Paragraph dialog box to adjust line spacing. *You can select from Single, 1.5 lines, and Double line spacing, or choose to customize the line spacing even more by selecting the At Least, Exactly, or Multiple option and entering a value in the By box.*

Indent a Paragraph Using the Formatting Toolbar

Click anywhere in the paragraph or select multiple paragraphs you want to indent, and then on the Formatting toolbar click the:

◆ Increase Indent button to move the entire paragraph to the right one half inch at a time.

◆ Decrease Indent button to move the entire paragraph to the left one half inch at a time.

Indent a Paragraph Using a Dialog Box

(1) Select the paragraph(s) you want to indent.

(2) Click the Format menu, click Paragraph, and then click the Indents And Spacing tab.

(3) Click the Left or Right up or down arrow to ajust the indent amount.

(4) If necessary, select First Line or Hanging in the Special pop-up menu, and then click the By up or down arrow to adjust the indent amount.

(5) Click OK.

Increase Indent button

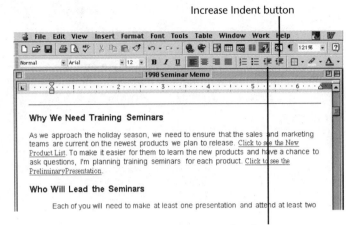

Decrease Indent button

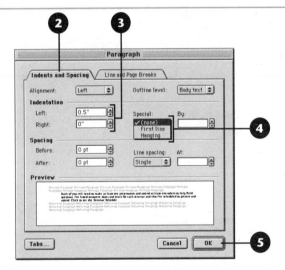

6

Setting Margins

Margins are the blank space between the edge of a page and the text. The default setting for Word documents is 1.25 inches on the left and right, and 1 inch on the top and bottom. You can set new margins for an entire section or document by dragging the margin boundaries on the rulers. To set new margins for the document from the current location of the insertion point forward, use the Page Setup dialog box.

SEE ALSO

See "Displaying Rulers" on page 86 for information about displaying and hiding the horizontal and vertical rulers.

SEE ALSO

See "Setting Paragraph Indents" on page 88 for information on adjusting the alignment of text in a paragraph.

Set Margins Using the Horizontal or Vertical Rulers

1 Click the Page Layout View button or the Normal View button.

2 Position the pointer over a margin boundary on the horizontal or vertical ruler.

3 If you want, press and hold the Option key while dragging the margin boundry to display the measurement of the text area.

4 Drag the left, right, top, or bottom margin boundary to a new position.

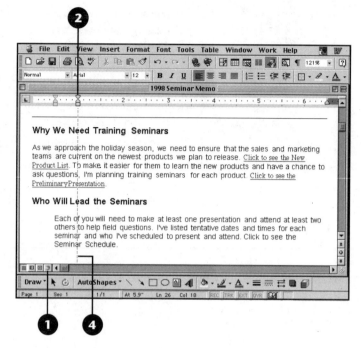

TIP

What are mirror margins?
The Mirror Margins option allows you to adjust the left and right margins, so that, when you print on both sides of a page, the inside margins of facing pages are the same width and the outside margins are the same width.

TIP

Margins for headers and footers. *Word measures the distance from the top and bottom of the page to the header or footer. Preview your document to make sure there is enough room to print the header text on the page; if not, adjust the margins here.*

SEE ALSO

See "Inserting New Pages and Sections" on page 94 for information about dividing your document into sections.

Set Margins Using a Dialog Box

1. If you want to change margins for only part of the document, click in the paragraph where you want the new margins to begin. (When changing margins for the entire document, it doesn't matter where the insertion point is located.)

2. Click the Format menu, click Document, and then click the Margins tab.

3. Type new margin measurements (in inches) in the Top, Bottom, Left, or Right boxes.

4. Check your changes in the Preview box.

5. Click the Apply To pop-up menu, and then select Whole Document or This Point Forward.

6. To make the new margin settings the default for all new Word documents, click Default and then click Yes.

7. Click OK.

You don't have to type the inch (") symbol.

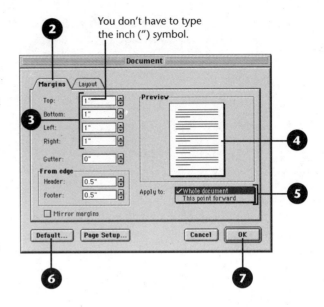

Working with Templates

A *template* is a special document in which you can store styles, text and formatting to use in other documents. You can use your own or any of Word's predefined templates as the basis of a new document, or attach template styles to the current document. When you attach a template to an existing document, you make the template styles available to only that document.

TIP

You are probably using the Normal template. *By default, all Word documents use the Normal template, which automatically formats text in 10-point Times, and offers three different heading styles.*

SEE ALSO

See "Creating and Modifying a Style" on page 96 for information on styles.

Save a Document as a Template

1. Open a new or existing document.

2. Add the text, graphics, and formatting you want to appear in all new documents based on this template. Adjust margin settings and page size, and create new styles as necessary.

3. Click the File menu, and then click Save As.

4. Click the Save File As Type pop-up menu, and then select Document Template.

5. Make sure the Templates folder (usually located in the Microsoft Office 98 folder on the hard drive or one of its subfolders) appears in the pop-up menu.

6. Type a name for the new template in the File Name box.

7. Click Save. You can open the template, and make and save other changes just as you would any other document.

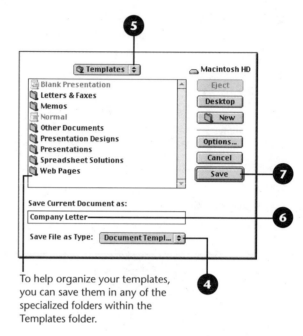

To help organize your templates, you can save them in any of the specialized folders within the Templates folder.

Create a New Document from a Template

(1) Click the File menu, and then click New.

(2) Click the tab for the type of template you want.

(3) Double-click the icon for the template you want.

(4) Edit the template to create a new document.

(5) Click the Save button on the Standard toolbar and save your document.

If you save a template in the Templates folder, you'll find its icon on the General tab.

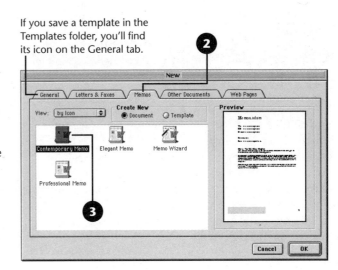

Apply a Template to an Existing Document

(1) Open the document to which you want to apply a new template.

(2) Click the Format menu, and then click Style Gallery.

(3) Click a template name to preview it.

(4) Click OK to add the template styles to the document.

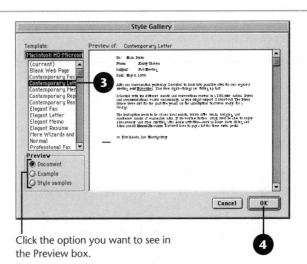

Click the option you want to see in the Preview box.

Inserting New Pages and Sections

When you fill a page, Word automatically inserts a page break and begins a new page. As you add or delete text, this *soft page break* will move. To start a new page before you reach the end of the current one, you need to manually insert a page break (called a *hard page break* because it doesn't shift as you edit text). A *section* is a mini-document within a document; you can format it with different margins, page orientation, and so on, no matter how the rest of the document looks.

Work with a section. *Open or create a multipage document, add a section break in the middle, and then format each section differently. Then use different margins and line spacing for each section and print the results.*

Insert and Delete a Page Break

(1) Click where you want to insert a hard page break.

(2) Click the Insert menu, and then click Break.

(3) Click the Page Break option button.

To insert a column break, click the Column Break option button.

(4) Click OK.

(5) Click the page break and then press Delete or Del to delete it.

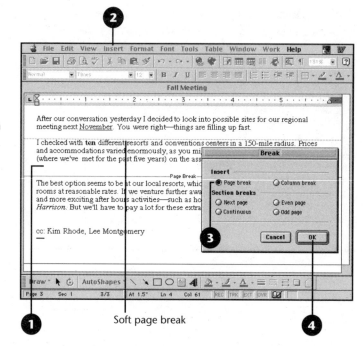

Soft page break

Insert and Delete a Section Break

(1) Click where you want to insert a section break.

(2) Click the Insert menu, and then click Break.

(3) Under Section Breaks, click the break option you want.

(4) Click OK.

(5) Click the section break and then press Delete or Del to delete it.

Starts the section on a new page

Starts the section on the next even or odd page

Starts the section wherever the insertion point is located

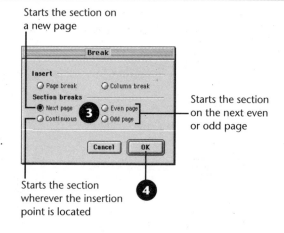

Applying a Style

A *style* is a collection of formatting settings you can apply to selected text. You can copy styles from selected text and apply them elsewhere in your document with the Format Painter. But the easiest way to use a style is to save it as part of a document or template. The style's name will then appear in the Style list box on the Formatting toolbar, ready for you to use whenever you like.

TIP

Paint a format in multiple locations. *Select the formatting you want to copy. Double-click the Format Painter button, and then drag the pointer over the text you want to format in each location. Click the Format Painter button again when you are finished.*

SEE ALSO

See "Working with Templates" on page 92 for information on applying predefined template styles to a document.

Copy a Style with the Format Painter

(1) Select the text with the formatting style you want to copy.

(2) Click the Format Painter button on the Standard toolbar.

(3) Select the text you want to format with the Format Painter pointer.

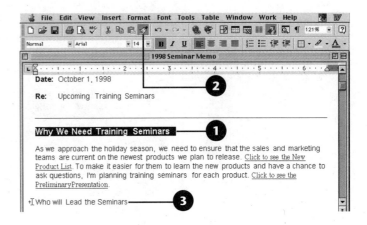

Change a Style Using the Style List

(1) Make sure the template with the styles you want is attached to the current document.

(2) Select the text you want to format.

(3) Click the Style drop-down arrow on the Formatting toolbar, and then select the style you want to use.

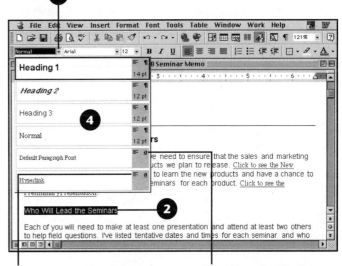

Indicates the style will affect the entire paragraph in which the insertion point is located

Indicates the style will affect only the selected text

6

Creating and Modifying a Style

Even though Word provides a variety of styles to choose from, you can create a new style or modify an existing style to better fit your needs. When you create a new style, you need to specify if the style applies to paragraphs or characters. Also, make sure you give the style a name that indicates the purpose of it. When you modify a style, you simply make adjustments to an existing one.

TIP

Use the List box to change style settings. *The List box in the Style dialog box provides three options: Styles In Use, All Styles, and User-Defined Styles. The styles listed in the Styles list box are based on the List option you choose.*

Create a New Style

1. Select the text whose formatting you want to save as a style.

2. Click the Format menu, click Style, and then click New.

3. Type a short, descriptive name that describes the style's purpose.

4. Click the Style Type pop-up menu, and then select Paragraph if you want the style to include the line spacing and margins of the selected text, or select Character if you want the style to include only formatting, such as font type, bold, and so on.

5. Click the Add To Template check box to add the new style to the current template.

6. Click OK.

7. Click Apply or click Close.

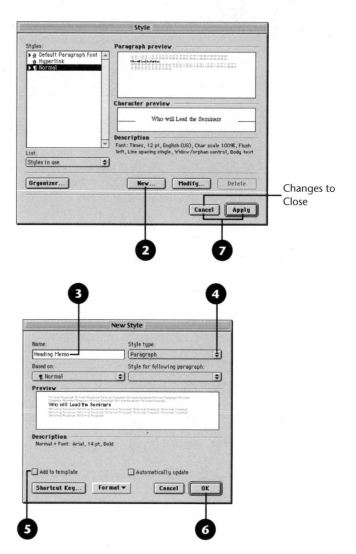

Changes to Close

Modify a style quickly. *Try to modify the style by adding italics. Select the text with the Title style, click the Italic button on the Formatting toolbar, click the Style drop-down arrow, click Title, click Update The Style To Reflect Recent Changes option button, and then click OK.*

Create a style quickly. *Try creating a heading style that centers and bolds text. Select the text, and then click the Center button and the Bold button on the Formatting toolbar. Then highlight the style name in the Style box on the Formatting toolbar. Type a short, descriptive name, such as Titles, and then press Return. The style is now available for your document.*

See "Working with Templates" on page 92 for information about applying predefined template styles to a document.

Modify a Style

1 Click the Format menu, and then click Style.

2 In the Styles list box, click the style you want to modify.

3 Click Modify.

4 Click the Format pop-up menu, and then select the type of formatting you want to modify. To change character formatting, such as font type and boldface, click Font. To change line spacing and indents, click Paragraph.

5 In the next dialog box, select the formatting options you want, and then click OK.

6 Review the description of the style, and make other formatting changes as necessary.

7 Click OK.

8 Click Apply or click Close.

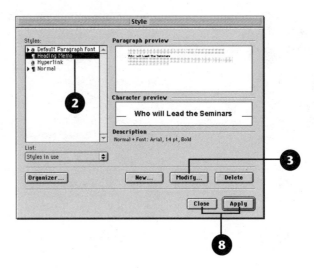

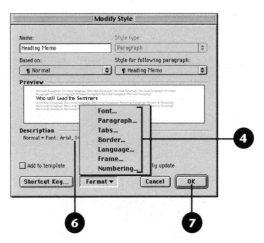

Creating Bulleted and Numbered Lists

The best way to draw attention to a list is to format it with bullets or numbers, a task Word can perform for you. Once you've created a bulleted or numbered list, you can change its character or number default style to one of Word's numerous pre-defined formats. For example, you can change a numerical list to an alphabetical list. If you move, insert, or delete items in a numbered list, Word will renumber the list sequentially for you.

Bullet button

Create a Bulleted List

1 Click where you want to create a bulleted list.

2 Click the Bullet button on the Formatting toolbar.

3 Type the first item in your list, and then press Return.

4 For each additional item in your list, type the item and press Return to insert a new bullet.

5 When you finish your list, click the Bullet button again to return to normal text.

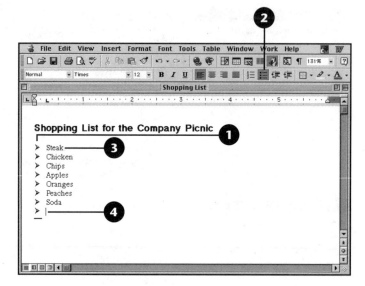

Create a Numbered List

1 Click where you want to create a numbered list.

2 Click the Numbering button on the Formatting toolbar.

3 Type the first item in your list, and then press Return.

4 For each additional item in your list, type the item and press Return to insert a new number.

5 When you finish your list, click the Numbering button again to return to normal text.

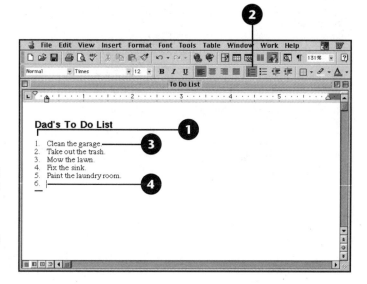

Numbering button

TIP

Change spacing between character and text. *You can change the amount of space between the bullet or number and the text. Click Customize in the Bullets And Numbering dialog box, and then change the Bullet (or Number) Position and Text Position options to specify where you want the bullet (or number) to appear and how much to indent the text.*

SEE ALSO

See "Setting Paragraph Indents" on page 88 for information on using the Increase Indent and Decrease Indent buttons.

Switch Between a Bulleted List and a Numbered List

1 Select the list.

2 Click the Bullet or Numbering button on the Formatting toolbar.

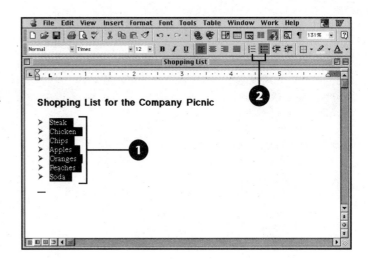

Change Bullet or Numbering Styles

1 Select the bulleted or numbered list.

2 Click the Format menu, and then click Bullets And Numbering.

3 Click either the Bulleted tab or the Numbered tab.

4 Click a predefined format.

5 If you want, click Customize and change the predefined format style and position settings.

6 Click OK.

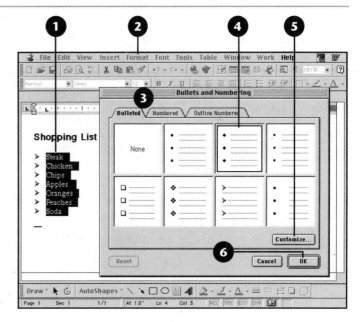

Creating a Form Letter

Mail merge is the process of combining names and addresses stored in a data file with a main document (usually a form letter) to produce customized documents. There are four main steps to merging. First, you need to tell Word what document you want to use as the main document. Next, you need to create a data file. Then you need to create the main document. Finally, you need to merge the two.

Select a Main Document

1. Open a new document or an existing document you want to use as the main document.

2. Click the Tools menu, and then click Mail Merge.

3. Click Create and then select the type of document you want to create.

4. Click Active Window to make the current document the main document.

5. Make sure the merge type and the main document are correct.

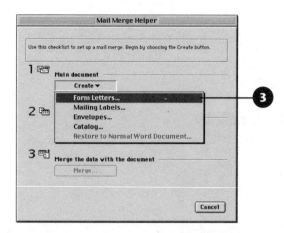

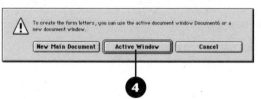

TIP

Use exisiting data to create a form letter. *You can easily select an existing data file instead by clicking the Get Data button in the Mail Merge Helper and then clicking Open Data Source.*

Create a Data File

1. If the Mail Merge Helper dialog box isn't open, click the Tools menu, and then click Mail Merge.

2. Click Get Data, and then select Create Data Source.

3. To delete an unwanted field name, click it in the Field Names In Header Row list, and then click Remove Field Name.

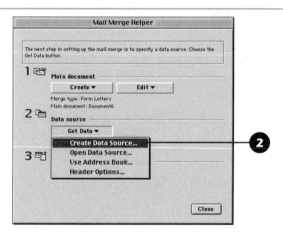

TIP

What are field names?

Information in a data file is stored in fields, labeled with one-word names such as FirstName, LastName, City, and so on. You insert field names in the main document as blanks, or placeholders. When you merge the data file and main document, Word fills in the blanks with the correct information.

SEE ALSO

See "Merging a Form Letter with Data" on page 102 for information on creating a main document and merging a main document with a data file.

4 To insert a new field name, type the field name in the Field Name box, and then click Add Field Name.

5 Click OK.

6 In the Save As dialog box, save the data file (which so far only contains field names) as you would any other document.

7 Click the Edit Data Source button to enter information into the data file.

8 Enter information for each field in the Data Form for one person or company record. Press Tab to move from one box to the next.

9 When you've typed all the data for one person or company, click Add New and repeat step 8.

10 After you've entered all the records you want, click OK.

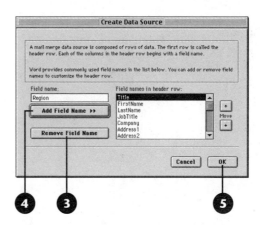

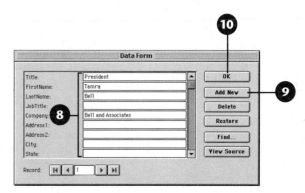

Merging a Form Letter with Data

Once you have selected a main document and have created a data file, you need to insert the merge fields in the main document. The merge fields are those available in the data file you selected for this merge. When you insert a merge field in your main document, make sure you insert the appropriate punctuation and spacing so the data will merge correctly into the fields and document text.

Mail Merge Helper button

SEE ALSO

See "Creating a Form Letter" on page 100 for information on selecting a main document and creating a data file.

Create the Main Document

1 If you don't see your main document displayed along with the Mail Merge toolbar, click the Tools menu, click Mail Merge, click Edit, and then click the name of your main document.

2 If necessary, type and format the text you want to appear in every document, but leave the information that will vary from letter to letter blank (for example, type "Dear Mr. :").

3 Click in the document where you want to insert a field name.

4 Click the Insert Merge Field button on the Mail Merge toolbar, and then click the field name.

5 When you're finished inserting field names, click the Save button on the Standard toolbar, and then save the document just as you would any other document.

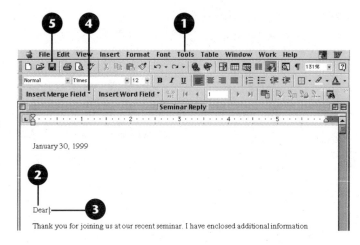

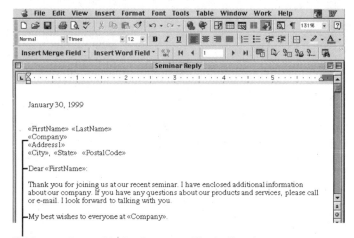

Field names inserted in the document. Word will replace these field names with names and addresses from the data file when you perform the merge.

Merge To New
Document button

Merge the Main Document and the Data File

1 Make sure the main document (with field names inserted) and the Mail Merge toolbar appear.

2 Click the Merge To New Document button on the Mail Merge toolbar.

3 Save and print the new document.

4 Close the new document.

5 Close the main document.

6 Click Yes if you are asked to save changes to the data file or the main document.

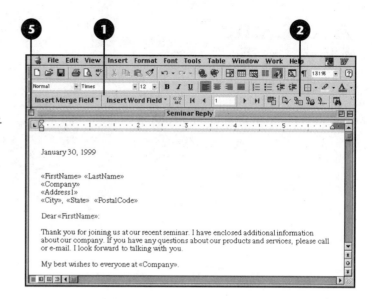

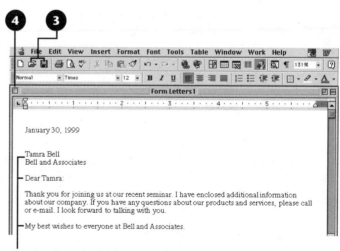

Word replaces the field names with the appropriate information from the data file.

Addressing Envelopes and Labels

Word can print an address on an envelope. Delivery and return addresses can contain text, graphics, and barcodes. Word can print two types of codes on an envelope: the POSTNET barcode, which is a machine-readable representation of a U.S. zip code and the delivery address; and the FIM-A code, which identifies the front of a courtesy reply envelope. You can also print an address on a mailing label. You can print a single label or multiple labels.

SEE ALSO

See "Creating a Form Letter" on page 100 for information on printing multiple envelopes or labels with different addresses by merging documents.

TIP

Format the address. *Select the address text, Control-click the text, and then click Font.*

Address and Print an Envelope

1. Click the Tools menu, and then click Envelopes And Labels.

2. Enter the address information, or click the Address Book button.

3. To select an envelope size, type of paper, feed method, and barcodes, click Options.

4. Insert the envelope in the printer as shown in the Feed Method box, click Print, and then click Print again.

Address and Print Mailing Labels

1. Click the Tools menu, and then click Envelopes And Labels.

2. Enter the address information, or click the Address Book button.

3. Click the Full Page or Single Label print option button.

4. To select a label type, click Options.

5. Insert the sheet of labels in the printer, click Print, and then click Print again.

Click to add delivery address to the active document.

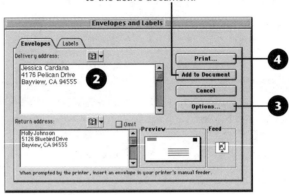

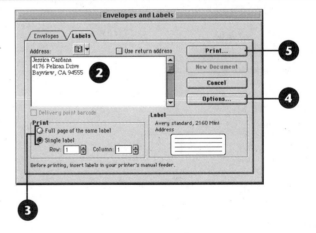

Enhancing a Document with Word 98

O nce you've mastered the basics of word processing with Microsoft Word 98, you can try some of the more advanced features. In most cases, there's more than one way to perform tasks such as creating tables or adding clip art. To save you time, this book focuses on the fastest and easiest methods.

Enhancing Your Document

After you've created your basic document, take a moment to consider how you can enhance its appearance and communicate its message more effectively. For example, you could draw attention to important text and data or clarify the details of a complicated paragraph by using a table. If your document is a brochure or newsletter, you'll probably want to take advantage of Word's desktop publishing features that allow you to format text in columns, as well as add headlines instantly.

Several Word features—among them, templates, styles, and the Find and Replace commands—are designed to help you work faster and more efficiently. You can use any of Word's predefined templates and styles, or create your own, to serve as the foundation for your routine documents.

Creating Headers and Footers

A *header* is text that is printed in the top margin of every page. *Footer* text is printed in the bottom margin. Common information to put in headers and footers includes your name, the name of your document, the date the document is printed, and page numbers. Rather than typing this text you can use the Insert AutoText pop-up menu on the Header And Footer toolbar. If you've divided your document into sections, you can create different headers and footers for each section.

TIP

Use Alignment buttons to change text placement.
Instead of using the default tab stops, you can use the Alignment buttons on the Formatting toolbar. For example, you might want just your company name aligned on the right margin of the header.

Create and Edit Headers and Footers

(1) Click the View menu, and then click Header And Footer.

Word switches to page layout view to display the header text area.

(2) If necessary, click the Switch Between Header And Footer button on the Header And Footer toolbar to display the footer text area.

(3) Click in the header or footer area, and then type the text you want.

(4) To insert common phrases, click the Insert AutoText button on the Header And Footer toolbar, and then click the AutoText entry you want to insert.

(5) Edit and format the header or footer text as you would any other text.

(6) When you're finished, click the Close button on the Header And Footer toolbar.

Document text appears in light gray, indicating that it is not available for editing.

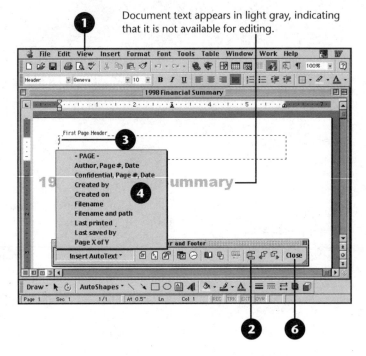

Use default tab stops to adjust header and footer text. *Headers and footers have three default tab stops. The first, on the far left, aligns text on the left margin. The second, in the middle, centers text. The third, on the far right, aligns text on the right margin.*

See "Inserting New Pages and Sections" on page 94 for more information on dividing a document into sections.

See "Settings Margins" on page 90 for information about settng margins for headers and footers.

Create section headers and footers. *Divide a multipage document into sections, and then create different headers and footers for each section.*

Create Different Headers and Footers for Different Pages

(1) Click the View menu, and then click Header And Footer.

(2) Click the Document Layout button on the Header And Footer toolbar.

(3) Click the Layout tab.

(4) To create a unique header or footer for the first page of the document, click the Different First Page check box. To create different headers or footers for odd and even pages, click the Different Odd And Even check box.

(5) Click OK.

(6) Click the Show Previous button and Show Next button to move from one header to the next, and enter and format the text you want in the remaining headers and footers.

(7) To move between the header and footer, click the Switch Between Header And Footer button.

(8) Click the Close button on the Header And Footer toolbar.

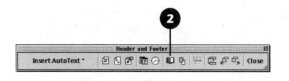

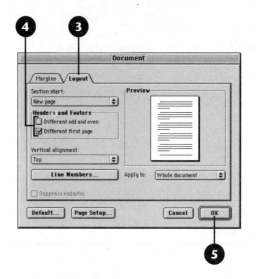

Inserting Page Numbers, the Date, and Time

To better document your work, you can have every page in the document numbered. Inserting this information in a header or footer is a standard way of keeping track of your work. When you insert the date and time, Word uses your computer's internal calendar and clock as its source. Numbering the pages in a document is also an important tracking tool, even if the document is only a few pages. You can insert the total number of pages in a document as well as the individual page numbers.

SEE ALSO

See "Creating Headers and Footers" on page 106 for information on headers and footers.

Insert Page Numbers, the Date, or Time

1. Click the View menu, and then click Header And Footer.

2. Click in the header or footer where you want to insert the page number, the date, or time. Remember to use the Tab key to move to the next tab stop.

3. Click the appropriate button or buttons on the Header And Footer toolbar.

    You can enter text along with the header and footer information. For example, you can type the word "Page."

4. If necessary, select the date, time, or page number, and then format it as you would any other text.

5. To delete any item, select it and then press Delete.

6. When you're done, click the Close button on the Header And Footer toolbar.

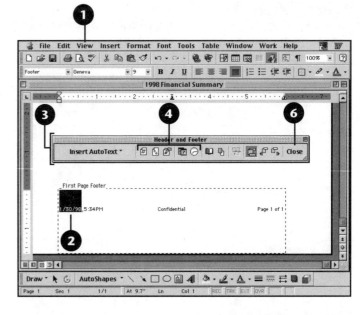

Insert Page Number button
Click to insert the correct page number on each page.

Insert Date button
Click to insert the current date from your computer's calendar.

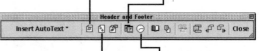

Insert Number Of Pages button
Click to insert the total number of pages in the document.

Insert Time button
Click to insert the current time from your computer's clock.

Inserting Symbols and AutoText

Being able to insert just the right symbol or character in your document is a good example of Word's extensive destop publishing capabilities. Your document's professional appearance will not be compromised by having to pencil in an arrow (→) or a mathmematical symbol. Inserting a symbol or special character is easy; position the pointer where you want to insert the symbol or character, choose the Symbol command and select a symbol or character.

Insert Symbols and Special Characters

1. Click in the document where you want to insert a symbol or character.

2. Click the Insert menu, and then click Symbol.

3. Click the Symbols tab or the Special Characters tab.

4. In the Symbols tab, click the Font pop-up menu, and then select a font.

5. Click the symbol or character you want.

6. Click Insert.

7. Click Close.

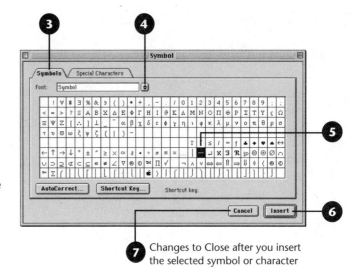

7 Changes to Close after you insert the selected symbol or character

Insert AutoText

1. Click in the document where you want to insert text using AutoText.

2. Click the Insert menu, and then point to AutoText.

3. Point to the type of AutoText you want to insert.

4. Click the AutoText you want to insert.

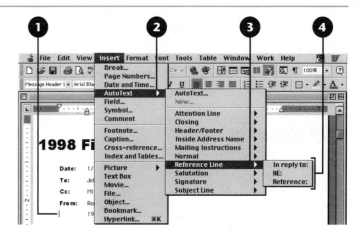

Inserting Comments

Comments in a document are like electronic adhesive notes. You can use them to get feedback from other readers before finalizing a document, or to remind yourself of revisions and changes you plan to make to the document in the future.

Insert a Comment

1. Click in the document where you want to insert a comment.
2. Click the Insert menu, and then click Comment to open the comment pane.
3. Type your comment in the comment pane next to the code.
4. If you want, click the Comments From drop-down arrow to view the comments made by you or other reviewers.
5. Click Close.

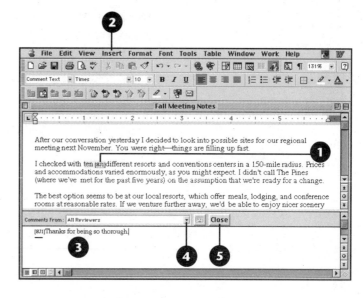

Read and Delete a Comment

1. Click the View menu, and then click Comments.
2. Read the comment associated with the first comment code.
3. To display the next comment, click the Next Comment button on the Reviewing toolbar.
4. To delete the selected comment, click the Delete Comment button on the Reviewing toolbar.
5. Click Close.

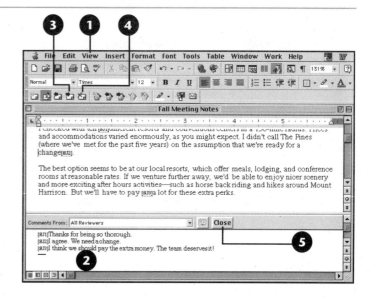

Tracking Changes

When a document is going to be edited by you or by others in your workgroup, you can track the changes and set up the document for various ways of marking your changes. If you need feedback on the basic ideas in a document, compile the main points of your document in a *summary*, which you can distribute to your colleagues, instead of the entire document.

Mark Your Changes

1. Click the View menu, point to Toolbars, and then click Reviewing to display the toolbar.

2. Click the Save Version button to save an unedited copy of the document.

3. Click the Track Changes button.

4. Edit the text.

5. Click the Previous Change button or the Next Change button to view changes.

6. Click the Accept button or Reject button to manage the changes.

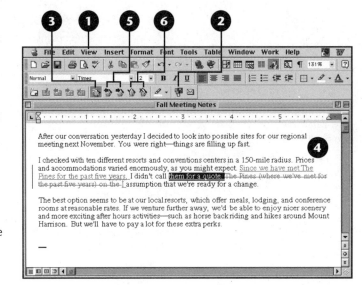

Summarize Your Document

1. Click the Tools menu, then click AutoSummarize.

2. Choose the type of summary option you want.

3. Click the Percent Of Original pop-up menu, and select the best length for your summary.

4. Click OK.

5. Read your summary carefully and edit it as necessary.

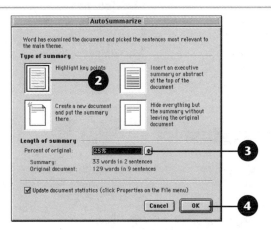

Creating a Table

A *table* organizes information neatly into rows and columns. The intersection of a row and column is called a *cell*. You enter text into cells just as you would anywhere else in a document, except that pressing the Tab key moves you from one cell to the next. You can also create a table from exisiting text. If, for example, you have aligned related information using tabs and you then decide to use a table to present the information more efficiently, you can convert the text to a table. If you decide not to use the table, you can convert a table to text just as easily.

TIP

Draw a custom table. *Click the Tables And Borders button on the Standard toolbar, click the Draw Table button on the Tables And Borders toolbar, draw a rectangle to create a table, and the draw lines to create cells.*

Create a Table Quickly

1. Move the insertion point to the beginning of a new paragraph.

2. Click the Insert Table button on the Standard toolbar.

3. Drag to select the appropriate number of rows and columns.

4. Release the mouse button to insert a blank grid in the document. The insertion point is in the first cell, ready for you to begin typing.

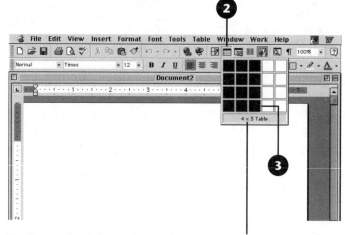

The first number indicates the number of rows, the second the number of columns. This 4x3 table will have four rows and three columns.

Create a Table from Existing Text

1. Select one or more lines of text separated by tabs, paragraphs, or commas.

2. Click the Table menu, and then click Convert Text To Table.

3. Select the number of columns and rows.

4. Click the option to separate text at paragraphs, tabs, commas, or other.

5. Click OK.

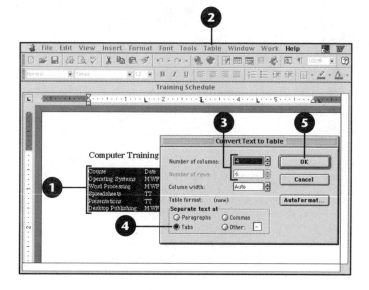

Entering Text in a Table

Once you create your table or convert text to a table, you need to enter (or add) text in each cell. You will probably use the first row in the table for your column headings, or list the headings down the first column on the left. You also need to know how to move around the table to make entering text easy. Knowing how to select the rows and columns of a table is also essential to working with the table itself.

TIP

Expand the row height as you type. *As you type in a cell, the text will wrap to the next line according to the width of the column; in other words, the height of a row expands as you enter text that is greater than the width of the column.*

TIP

Delete cell contents. *Select the cells whose contents you want to delete, click the Edit menu, and the click Clear.*

Enter Text and Move Around a Table

The insertion point shows where text you type will appear in a table. After you type text in a cell:

◆ Press Return to start a new paragraph within that cell.

◆ Press Tab to move the insertion point to the next cell to the right (or to the first cell in the next row).

◆ Use the arrow keys or click anywhere in the table to move the insertion point to a new location.

Select Table Elements

Refer to the table for methods to select table elements, including:

◆ The entire table

◆ One or more rows and columns

◆ One or more cells

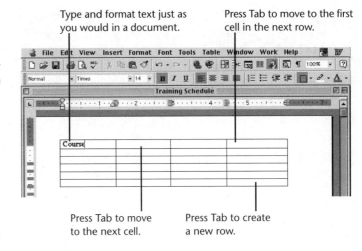

Type and format text just as you would in a document.

Press Tab to move to the first cell in the next row.

Press Tab to move to the next cell.

Press Tab to create a new row.

SELECTING TABLE ELEMENTS	
To Select	**Do This**
The entire table	Click in the table, click the Table menu, and then click Select Table.
One or more rows	Click in the left margin next to the row you want to select, and then drag to select more rows.
One or more columns	Click just above the column (a down arrow appears) you want to select, and then drag to select more columns.
The row or column with the insertion point	Click the Table menu, and then click either Select Row or Select Column.
A single cell	Drag a cell or triple-click a cell.
More than one cell	Click a cell and then drag to select more cells.

7

Modifying a Table

After you create a table or begin to enter text in one, you might want to add more rows or columns to accommodate the text you are entering in the table. When you add a row, you select the row above which you want the new, blank row to appear. When you add a column, you select the column to the left of which you want the new, blank column to appear. When you want to insert more than one row or column, select that number of rows and columns first. For example, if you want to insert two rows, select two rows first. When you delete rows and columns from a table, the table aligns itself.

Insert Columns button

Insert Additional Rows

1 Select the row above which you want the new rows to appear.

2 Drag down to select the number of rows you want to insert.

3 Click the Insert Rows button on the Standard toolbar.

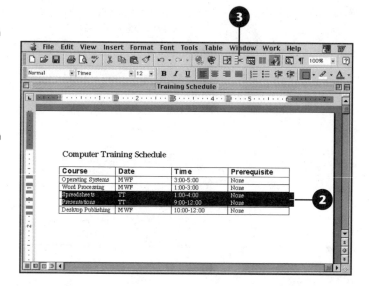

Insert Additional Columns

1 Select the column to the left of which you want the new columns to appear.

2 Drag right to select the number of columns you want to insert.

3 Click the Insert Columns button on the Standard toolbar.

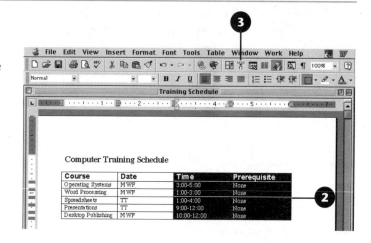

Delete Rows and Columns

(1) Select the rows or columns you want to delete.

(2) Click the Table menu, and then click Delete Rows or Delete Columns.

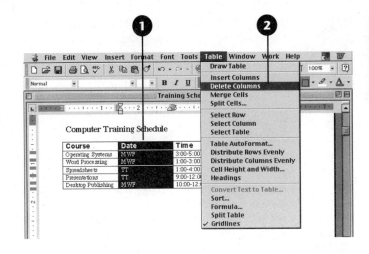

Adjust Row Height and Column Widths

(1) Move the mouse pointer over the boundary of the row or column you want to adjust until it changes into a resizing pointer.

(2) Drag the boundary to adjust the row or column to the size you want.

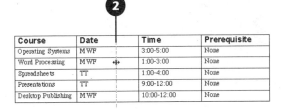

Adjusting Table Elements

Often there is more to modifying a table than adding or deleting rows or columns; you need to make each row or column just the right size to accommodate the text you are entering in the table. For example, you might have a title in the first row of a table that is longer than the first cell in that row. To spread the title across the top of the table, you can *merge*, or combine, the cells together to form one long cell. Sometimes to indicate a division in a topic, you will also need to *split*, or divide, a cell into two. Moreover, the width of a column and height of a row can also be modified to better suit your needs.

Merge and Split Table Cells

◆ To merge two or more cells into a single cell, select the cells you want to merge, click the Table menu, and then click Merge Cells.

◆ To split a cell into multiple cells, click in the cell you want to split, click the Table menu, and then click Split Cells. Type the number of rows or columns (or both) you want to split the selected cell into, and then click OK.

Before merging cells
The three cells in this row will be combined into one.

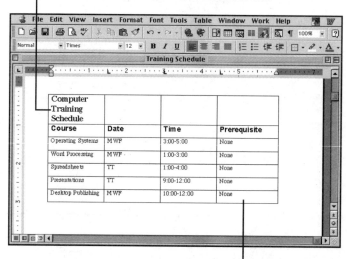

Before a splitting cell
This cell will be divided into two cells.

Three cells merged into one

Computer Training Schedule			
Course	**Date**	**Time**	**Prerequisite**
Operating Systems	M WF	3:00-5:00	None
Word Processing	M WF	1:00-3:00	None
Spreadsheets	TT	1:00-4:00	None
Presentations	TT	9:00-12:00	None
Desktop Publishing	M WF	10:00-12:00	None	

Single cell split into two

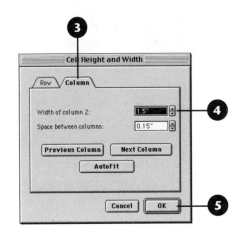

TIP

Adjust column text with AutoFit. *If you can't decide the appropriate widths for the columns in your table, click the AutoFit button, and Word will adjust the columns to fit the longest entry in each column.*

SEE ALSO

See "Formatting a Table" on page 118 for information on changing the look of a table.

TIP

Indent a table from the left edge of the document. *Click in the table, click the Table menu, click Cell Height And Width, click the Row tab, enter an inch measurement in the Indent From Left box, and then click OK.*

TIP

Change table alignment in the document. *Click in the table, click the Table menu, click Cell Height And Width, click the Row tab, click the Left, Center, or Right option button, and then click OK.*

Adjust Cell or Column Width

1. Select the cells or columns you want to change.

2. Click the Table menu, and click Cell Height And Width.

3. Click the Column tab.

4. Click the up and down arrow to select an inch measurement or Auto.

5. Click OK.

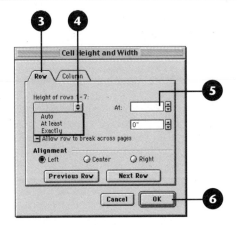

Adjust Cell or Row Height

1. Select the cells or rows you want to change.

2. Click the Table menu, and click Cell Height And Width.

3. Click the Row tab.

4. Click Exactly or At Least in the Height Of Rows box.

5. Click the At up and down arrow to specify an inch measurement.

6. Click OK.

Formatting a Table

Word makes it easy for you to format your table. You can change the alignment of the text in the cells (by default, text aligns on the left of a cell and numbers align on the right). If changing the alignment isn't enough, you can use the Table AutoFormat dialog box to format your table. This dialog box provides a variety of predesigned table formats that you can apply to a selected table. If the AutoFormat offerings don't suit your needs, you can choose to add borders and shading manually. Borders and shading help to make printed tables easier to read and more attractive.

SEE ALSO

See "Adding Desktop Publishing Effects" on page 120 for information about manually adding borders and shading.

Format a Table Automatically

(1) Select the table you want to format, click the Table menu, and then select Table AutoFormat.

(2) Select a format from the Formats list.

(3) Preview the results.

(4) When you find a format you like, click OK to apply it.

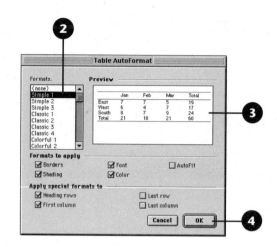

Align Text Within Cells Horizontally

(1) Select the cells, rows, or columns you want to align.

(2) Click the Align Left, Center, Align Right, or Justify button on the Formatting toolbar.

Centered text
Center column headings to make them stand out.

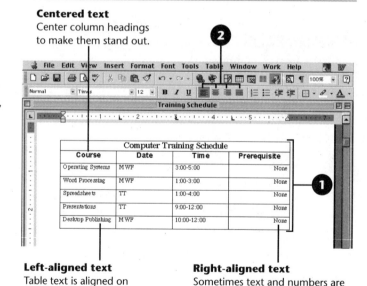

Left-aligned text
Table text is aligned on the left by default.

Right-aligned text
Sometimes text and numbers are easier to read when right-aligned.

7

Calculate the sum of a table column. *Display the Tables And Borders toolbar, click in the blank cell in the bottom row of the column that is to contain the sum of the cells above it, and then click the AutoSum button.*

Sort the entries in a table column. *Display the Tables And Borders toolbar, select the cells in the column you want to sort, and then click either the Sort Acending or Sort Decending button.*

Display or hide gridlines in a table. *Click the Table menu, and then click Gridlines to display the gridlines. To hide gridlines, click Gridlines again.*

Align Text Within Cells Vertically

1 Click the Tables And Borders button on the Standard toolbar to display the Tables And Borders toolbar.

2 Select the cells you want to vertically align.

3 Click an alignment button on the Tables And Borders toolbar.

Align Bottom button

Center Vertically button

Align Top button

Course	Date	Time	Prerequisite
Operating Systems	M WF	3:00-5:00	None
Word Processing	M WF	1:00-3:00	None
Spreadsheets	TT	1:00-4:00	None
Presentations	TT	9:00-12:00	None
Desktop Publishing	M WF	10:00-12:00	None

Change Text Direction Within Cells

1 Click the Tables And Borders button on the Standard toolbar to display the Tables And Borders toolbar.

2 Select the cells with the text you want to change direction.

3 Click the Change Text Direction button. (You might have to click the button two or three times to get the text direction you want.)

Button changes to show direction

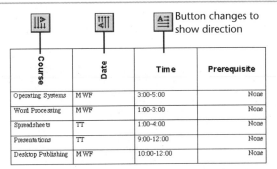

Course	Date	Time	Prerequisite
Operating Systems	M WF	3:00-5:00	None
Word Processing	M WF	1:00-3:00	None
Spreadsheets	TT	1:00-4:00	None
Presentations	TT	9:00-12:00	None
Desktop Publishing	M WF	10:00-12:00	None

Adding Desktop Publishing Effects

A few simple desktop publishing elements, such as drop caps and borders, can help you create newsletters and brochures that look like they've been professionally produced. These special elements look especially good when combined with pictures and text arranged in column format.

Tables And Borders button

Add Borders and Shading

1. Select the text you want to put a border around or shade.

2. Click the Tables And Borders button on the Standard toolbar.

3. Click the Line Style drop-down arrow, and then select a line pattern.

4. Click the Line Weight drop-down arrow, and then select a border line thickness.

5. Click the Border Color drop-down arrow, and then select a border color.

6. Click the Outside Border drop-down arrow, and then select the border you want to around the selected text.

7. Click the Shading Color drop-down arrow, and then select the background shading you want inside the border, if any.

8. Click the Close box on the Tables And Borders toolbar.

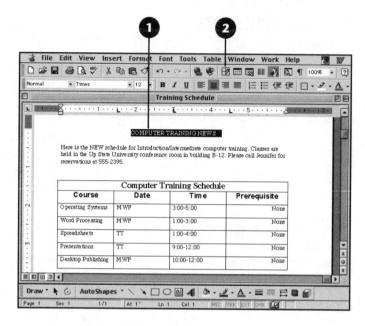

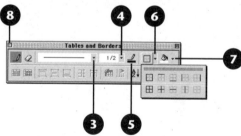

SEE ALSO

See "Drawing and Enhancing Objects" on page 38 for information on other desktop publishing elements. See "Arranging Text in Columns" on page 122 for information on formatting text in newspaper style columns.

TRY THIS

Create a newsletter. *Try creating a newsletter by first formatting the text in your document into columns. Then insert a picture and wrap the text around it. Finally, add drop caps to each paragraph, and a border and shading around important paragraphs. If you like, you could even add a WordArt headline.*

Add a Drop Cap to Text

1. Switch to page layout view.

2. Click in the paragraph where you want to create a drop cap.

3. Click the Format menu, and then click Drop Cap.

4. Click the Dropped icon to flow text around the drop cap or the In Margin icon to move the drop cap to the left margin.

5. If you want, click the Font pop-up menu, and then select a different font for the drop cap.

6. Click the Lines To Drop up or down arrow to adjust the height (in number of lines) for the drop cap.

7. Click the Distance From Text up or down arrow to adjust how far (in inches) you want the drop cap from the paragraph text.

8. Click OK.

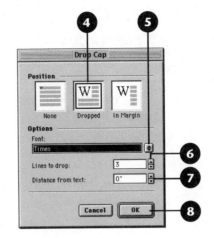

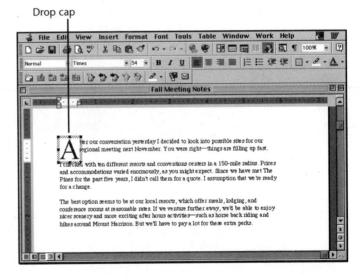

Drop cap

Arranging Text in Columns

Newspaper style columns can give newsletters and brochures a more polished look. Begin by using the Columns button to create the columns. Then choose among several column options to improve their appearance. Keep in mind that you can format an entire document or individual sections in columns. You must switch to page layout view to view the columns side by side on the screen.

TIP

Use the Formatting toolbar to align text in a column. *Select the columns you want to format, and then click the Align Left, Center, Align Right, or Justify button on the Formatting toolbar.*

Create Columns

1. Switch to page layout view.
2. Select the text you want to arrange in columns.
3. Click the Columns button on the Standard toolbar.
4. Drag to select the number of columns you want.

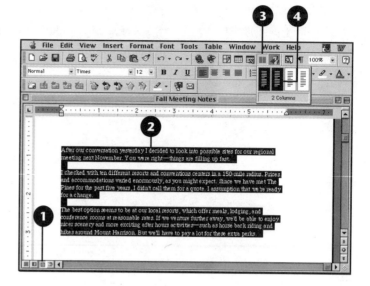

Modify Columns

1. Switch to page layout view.
2. Click the Format menu, and then click Columns.
3. Click a column format.
4. Specify the Width And Spacing you want.
5. Click OK.

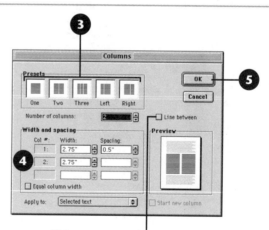

Click to separate columns with a thin vertical line.

8

Creating a Worksheet with Excel 98

If you're spending too much time number-crunching, rewriting financial reports, drawing charts, and searching for your calculator, you're probably eager to start using Microsoft Excel 98. This book teaches you to use Excel's most popular features so you can become productive immediately.

Microsoft Excel is a *spreadsheet program,* which is designed to help you record, analyze, and present quantitative information. Excel makes it easy to track and analyze sales, organize finances, create budgets, and accomplish a variety of business tasks in a fraction of the time it would take using pen and paper.

The file you create and save in Excel is called a *workbook.* It contains a collection of worksheets, which look similar to an accountant's ledger sheets, but using these worksheets, you can perform calculations and other tasks automatically. You can create a variety of workbooks that can be used for analysis and record keeping, such as:

◆ Monthly sales and expense reports

◆ Charts displaying annual sales data

◆ An inventory of products

◆ A payment schedule for an equipment purchase

Viewing the Excel Window

When you start Excel, the Excel program window opens with a blank workbook—ready for you to use. The Excel window contains everything you need to work with your Excel workbook.

The *title bar* contains the name of the active workbook.

Any data contained in the active cell appears on the *formula bar*.

All Excel commands are organized in menus on the *menu bar*.

The address of the currently selected (or active) cell appears in the *Name box*.

The *active cell* is the currently selected cell (its address appears in the Name box); you enter data in the active cell.

Each sheet contains a *tab* you can click to move from sheet to sheet; you can rename sheets to make it eaiser to remember what each one contains.

Frequently used Excel commands are available on *toolbar buttons*, which are organized in toolbars.

The intersection of a column and a row forms a *cell*; each cell has a unique address determined by the column letter and row number. For example, the cell B10 is the intersection of column B and row 10.

The *Office Assistant* automatically appears. You ask the Office Assistant questions about Excel tasks, and it provides helpful information based on your questions.

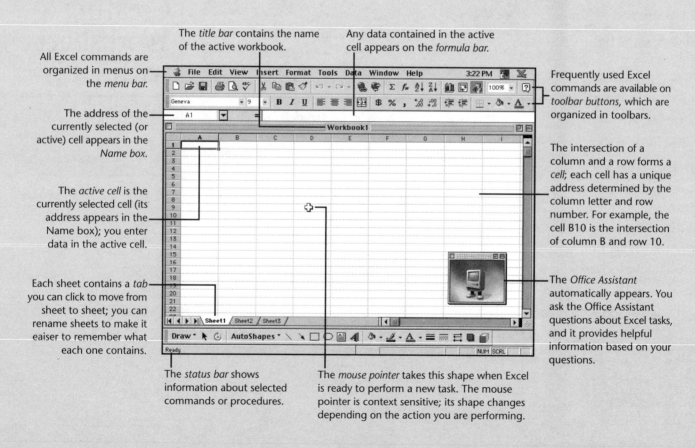

The *status bar* shows information about selected commands or procedures.

The *mouse pointer* takes this shape when Excel is ready to perform a new task. The mouse pointer is context sensitive; its shape changes depending on the action you are performing.

Moving Around the Workbook

You can move around a worksheet or workbook using your mouse or the keyboard. You might find that using your mouse to move from cell to cell is most convenient, while using various keyboard combinations is easier for covering large areas of a worksheet quickly. However, there is no one right way; whichever method feels the most comfortable is the one you should use.

SEE ALSO

See "Worksheet Basics" on page 132 for more information on sheet tabs.

Use the Mouse or Keyboard to Navigate

Using the mouse, you can navigate to:

◆ Another cell

◆ Another part of a worksheet

◆ Another worksheet

Using the keyboard, you can navigate to:

◆ The next cell by using the Tab key

◆ The first cell in the next row by using the Return key

To move from one cell to another, point to the cell you want to move to, and then click.

Mouse pointer

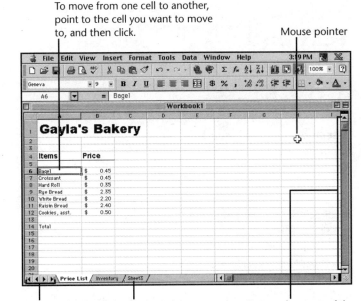

To see more sheet tabs *without* changing the active sheet, click a sheet scroll button.

To move from one worksheet to another, click the tab of the sheet you want to see.

To see other parts of the worksheet without changing the location of the active cell, click the horizontal and vertical scroll bars, or drag the scroll boxes.

Entering Text and Numbers in a Worksheet

Text labels turn a worksheet full of numbers into a meaningful report by clarifying the relationship between the numbers. You use labels to identify the data in the worksheet columns and rows. To help keep your labels consistent, Excel's *AutoComplete* feature automatically complete your entries based on labels you have entered previously. To enter a number as a label, for example, the year 2000, you type an apostrophe (') before the number. Then Excel does not use the number in its calculations. You can enter values as whole numbers, decimals, percentages, or dates. You can enter values using the numbers on the top row of your keyboard or the numeric keypad on the right.

Enter a Text Label

1 Click the cell where you want to enter a label.

2 Type a label. A label can include uppercase and lowercase letters, spaces, punctuation, and numbers.

3 Click the Enter button on the formula bar, or press Enter.

To enter the text and move to the next row, press Return.

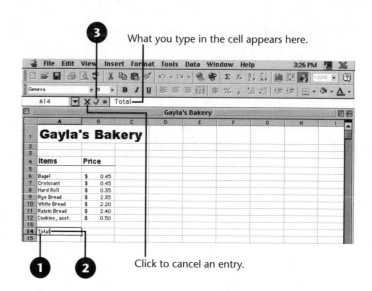

What you type in the cell appears here.

Click to cancel an entry.

Enter a Number as a Text Label

1 Click the cell where you want to enter a number as a label.

2 Type ' (an apostrophe). The apostrophe is a *label prefix* and does not appear in the worksheet.

3 Type a number value. Examples of numbers that you might use as labels include a year, a social security number, or a telephone number.

4 Click the Enter button on the formula bar, or press Enter.

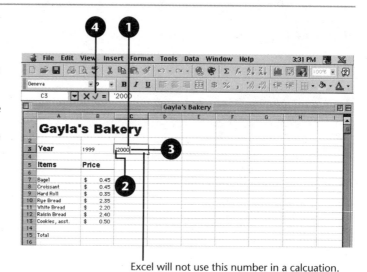

Excel will not use this number in a calcuation.

See "Creating a List" on page 157 for information on entering labels using the PickList.

Enter a Value

1 Click the cell where you want to enter a value.

2 Type a value. To simplify your data entry, type the values without commas and dollar signs and apply a numeric format to them later.

3 Click the Enter button on the formula bar, or press Enter.

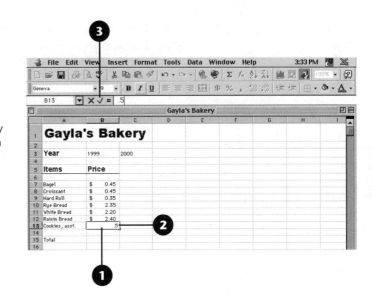

Enter a Text Label with AutoComplete

1 Begin typing an entry in a cell. If a previous entry in that column begins with the same characters, AutoComplete displays the entry.

2 Press Enter to accept the entry, or resume typing to ignore the AutoComplete suggestion, and then click the Enter button on the formula bar, or press Enter.

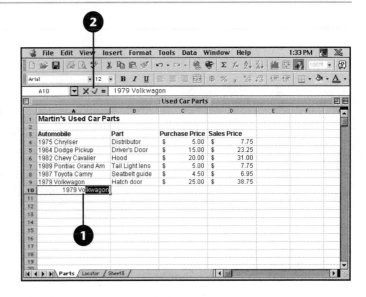

8

Editing Cell Contents

No matter how much you plan, you can count on having to make changes in a worksheet. Sometimes it's because you want to correct an error; other times you might want to incorporate new information, or see how your worksheet results would be affected by different conditions, such as higher sales, fewer units produced, or other variables. You edit data just as easily as you enter it, using the formula bar or directly editing the active cell.

SEE ALSO

See "Working with Cells" on page 129 for information on deleting a cell and clearing the contents of a cell.

Edit Cell Content

(1) Double-click the cell you want to edit. The insertion point appears within the cell.

The status bar now displays Edit instead of Ready in the lower left corner.

(2) If necessary, use the mouse pointer or the Home, End, and arrow keys to position the insertion point in the cell.

(3) If necessary, use any combination of the Delete and Del keys to erase unwanted characters.

(4) If necessary, type new characters.

(5) Click the Enter button on the formula bar to accept the edit, or click the Cancel button to cancel it.

Click to edit cell content using the formula bar.

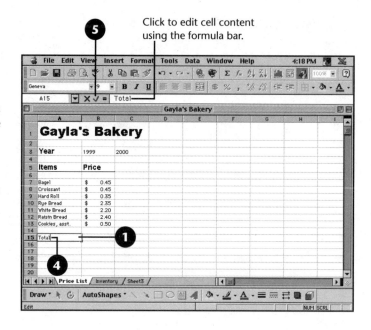

Working with Cells

You can insert new, blank cells anywhere in the worksheet, so you can enter new data or data you forgot to enter earlier, exactly where you want it. Inserting cells moves the remaining cells in the column or row in the direction of your choice and adjusts any formulas so they refer to the correct cells. You can also delete cells if you find you don't need them; deleting cells shifts the remaining cells to the left or up—just the opposite of inserting cells. When you delete a cell, Excel removes the actual cell from the worksheet.

TIP

Deleting a cell vs. clearing a cell. *Deleting a cell is different from clearing a cell; deleting removes the cells from the worksheet, and clearing removes only the cell content or format or both.*

Insert One or More Cells

1 Select the cell or cells where you want to insert the new cell(s).

2 Click the Insert menu, and then click Cells.

3 Click the option you want. If you want the contents of the cells to move right, click the Shift Cells Right option button, or if you want the contents of the cells to move to down, click the Shift Cells Down option button. Either way, two blank cells are now at the selected cells.

4 Click OK.

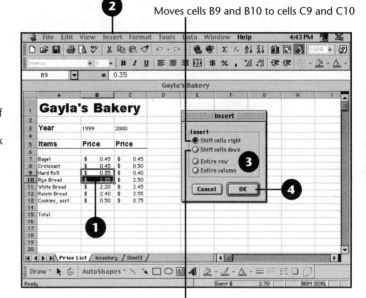

Moves cells B9 and B10 to cells C9 and C10

Moves cells B9 and B10 to cells B11 and B12

Delete One or More Cells

1 Select the cell or cells you want to delete.

2 Click the Edit menu, and then click Delete.

3 Click the option you want. If you want the remaining cells to move left, click the Shift Cells Left option button, or if you want the remaining cells to move up, click the Shift Cells Up option button.

4 Click OK.

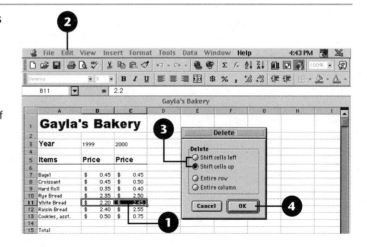

Selecting Multiple Cells

A *range* is one or more selected cells that you can edit, delete, format, print, or use as an argument in a formula just as you would a single cell. A range can consist of *contiguous* cells (where all the selected cells are adjacent to each other) or *noncontiguous* cells (where all the cells are not adjacent to each other). A range reference begins with the top leftmost cell in the range, followed by a colon (:), and ends with the cell address of the bottom rightmost cell in the range. To make working with ranges easier, Excel allows you to name them. The name "Sales," for example, is easier to remember than the coordinates B4:D10.

Select a Range

1. Click the first cell you want to include in the range.

2. Drag the mouse diagonally to the last cell you want to include the range. When a range is selected, the top, leftmost cell is surrounded by the active cell border while the additional cells are highlighted in black.

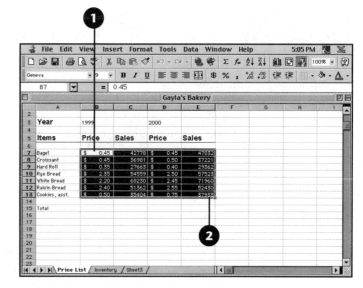

Select a Non-contiguous Range

1. Click the first cell you want to include in the range.

2. Drag the mouse diagonally to the last contiguous cell.

3. Press and hold the Command key and drag the mouse over the next group of cells you want in the range.

4. Repeat step 3 until all the cells are selected.

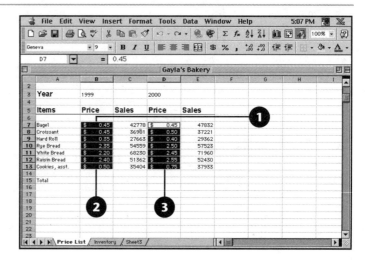

SEE ALSO

*See "Using Ranges in Formulas"
on page 142 for information on
creating formulas using range
names.*

Name a Range

1 Select a range you want to name.

2 Click the Name box on the formula bar.

3 Type a name for the range. A range name can include uppercase or lowercase letters, numbers, and punctuation. Try to use a simple name that reflects the type of information in the range, such as "Sales99."

4 Press Enter. The range name will appear in the Name box whenever you select the range.

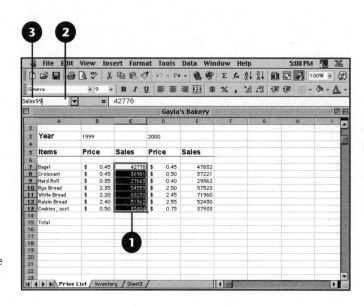

TRY THIS

**Go to a named range in a
worksheet.** *Press the F5 key
(or click the Edit menu, and
then click Go To) to see a list of
named ranges. Click the name
of the range you want to go to,
and then click OK.*

Select a Named Range

1 Click the Name box drop-down arrow on the formula bar.

2 Click the name of the range you want to select.

The range name appears in the Name box, and all cells included in the range are highlighted in the worksheet.

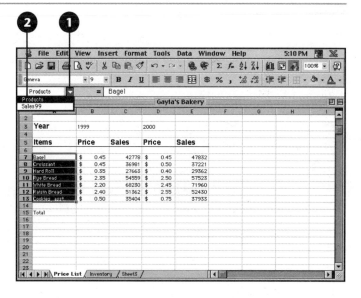

Worksheet Basics

Each new workbook you open has three workbook sheets. You can switch from sheet to sheet by clicking the sheet tab. Clicking the sheet tab makes that sheet *active*. Each of the sheets is named consecutively—Sheet1, Sheet2, and Sheet3. You can give a sheet a more meaningful name, and the size of the sheet tab automatically accommodates the name's length. You can add or delete sheets in a workbook. If you were working on a project that involved more than three worksheets, you could add sheets to a workbook rather than use multiple workbooks. That way, all your related information would be in one file. Deleting unused sheets saves disk space.

Select a Sheet

1. Click the sheet tab to make it the active worksheet.

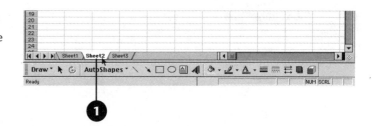

Name a Sheet

1. Double-click the sheet tab you want to name.

2. Type a new name. The current name, which is selected, is automatically replaced when you begin typing.

3. Press Return.

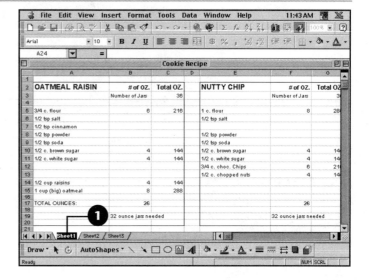

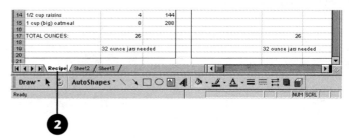

TIP

Use short sheet tab names to save screen space.

Because the size of a sheet tab enlarges to accommodate a longer name, using short names means more sheet tabs will be visible. This is especially important if a workbook contains several worksheets.

Insert a Worksheet

1 Click the sheet tab (or select any cell in a worksheet) to the right, or *in front of,* where you want to insert the new sheet.

2 Click the Insert menu, and then click Worksheet. A new worksheet will be inserted to the left of, or *behind,* the selected worksheet.

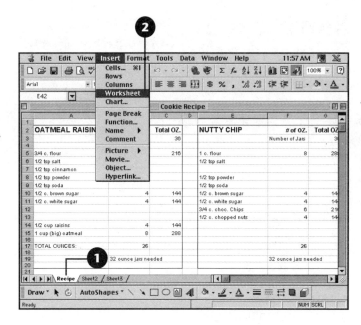

SEE ALSO

See "Moving and Copying a Worksheet" on page 134 for information on reorganizing sheets in a workbook.

Delete a Worksheet

1 Select any cell in the worksheet you want to delete.

2 Click the Edit menu, and then click Delete Sheet.

3 Click OK to confirm the deletion.

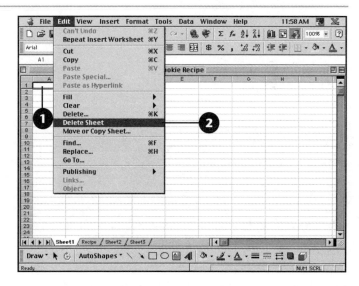

Moving and Copying a Worksheet

After adding several sheets to a workbook, you might want to reorganize them. You can easily move a sheet within a workbook or to another workbook by dragging it to a new location. You can also copy a worksheet within a workbook or to another workbook. Copying a worksheet is easier and often more convenient than having to reenter similar information in a new sheet. The ability to move and copy whole worksheets means you can have your workbooks set up exactly the way you want them, without having to do a lot of needless typing.

Move a Sheet

1. Click the sheet tab of the worksheet you want to move, and then press and hold the mouse button. The mouse pointer changes to a small sheet.

2. Drag the pointer to the right or in front of the sheet tab where you want to move the worksheet.

3. Release the mouse button.

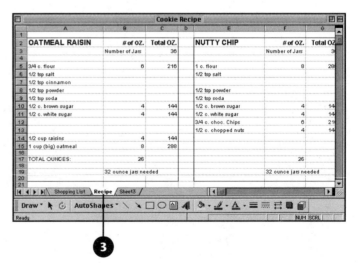

Copy a Sheet

1. Click the sheet tab of the worksheet you want to copy.

2. Click the Edit menu, and then click Move Or Copy Sheet.

3. If you want to copy the sheet to another workbook, click the To Book pop-up menu, and select that workbook. The sheets of the selected workbook appear in the Before Sheet box.

4. Click a sheet name in the Before Sheet list box. The copy will be inserted before this sheet.

5. Click the Create A Copy check box.

6. Click OK.

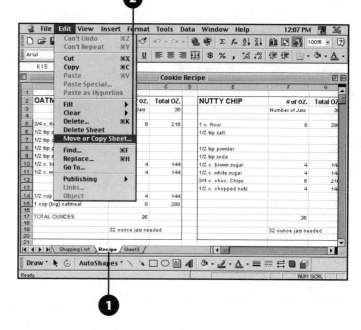

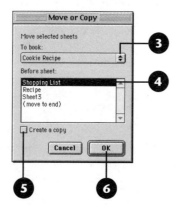

Inserting a Column or Row

You can insert blank columns and rows in a worksheet between columns or rows that are already filled without deleting and retyping anything. When you insert one or more columns, they are inserted to the left of the selected column. When you add one or more rows, they are inserted above the selected row. Excel repositions existing cells to accommodate the new columns and rows and adjusts any existing formulas so that they refer to the correct cells.

Insert a Column or Row

1 To insert a column, click anywhere in the column to the right of the location of the new column you want to insert.

To insert a row, click anywhere in the row immediately below the location of the row you want to insert.

2 Click the Insert menu, and then click Columns or Rows.

A column inserts to the left of the selected column or a row inserts above the selected row.

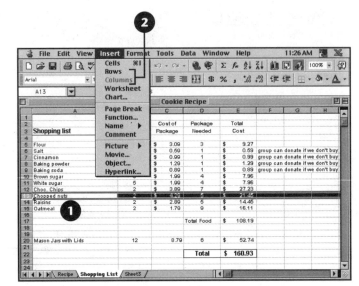

Insert Multiple Columns or Rows

1 To add multiple columns, drag to select the *column indicator* buttons for the number of columns to be inserted.

To add multiple rows, drag to select the *row indicator* buttons or the number of rows to be inserted.

2 Click the Insert menu, and then click Columns or Rows.

The number of columns or rows selected are inserted.

Column indicator button

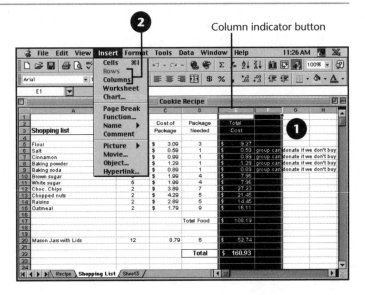

Previewing Page Breaks

If you want to print a worksheet that is larger than one page, Excel divides it into pages by inserting *automatic page breaks*. These page breaks are based on paper size, margin settings, and scaling option you set. You can change which rows or columns are printed on the page by inserting *horizontal* or *vertical page breaks*. In page break preview, you can view the page breaks and move them by dragging them to a different location on the worksheet.

Insert a Page Break

1 To insert a horizontal page break, click the column indicator to the right of the location where you want to insert a page break.

To insert a vertical page break, click the row indicator below the location where you want to insert a page break.

To start a new page, click the cell below and to the right of the location where you want a new page.

2 Click the Insert menu, and then click Page Break.

Page break inserts here

Automatic page break

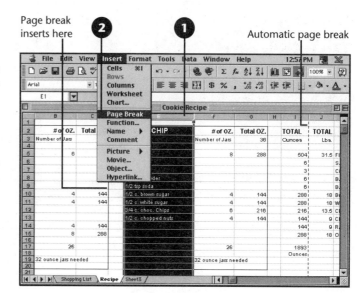

Preview and Move a Page Break

1 Click the View menu, and then click Page Break Preview.

2 Drag a page break to a new location.

3 When you're done, click the View menu, and then click Normal.

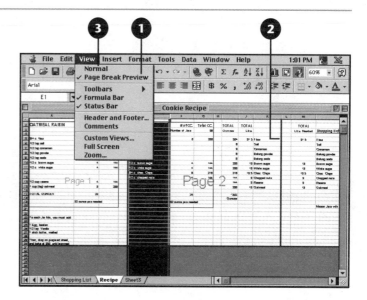

8

Printing a Worksheet

At some point you'll want to print out your work so you can distribute it to others or use it for other purposes. You can print all or part of any worksheet and control the appearance of many features, such as the gridlines that display on the screen, whether the column letters and row numbers display, or whether some columns and rows are repeated on each page.

Preview a Worksheet

1. Click the File menu, and then click Print Preview.

2. To preview the next page, click Next.

3. To zoom in a page, click Zoom. Click Zoom again to return to the previous view.

4. To change the margins, click Margins, and then drag a dotted margin line. Click Margins again to remove the dotted margin lines from Print Preview.

5. Click Close.

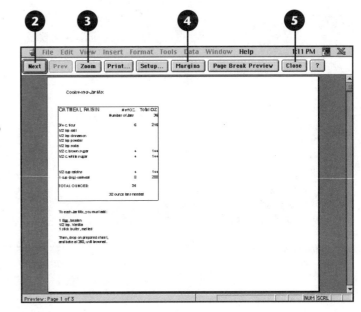

Print a Worksheet with Specific Options

1. Click the File menu, and then click Print.

2. Click the Printer pop-up menu, and then select the printer you want.

3. Specify the copies, pages, and page source you want to use.

4. Click the pop-up menu, and then select Microsoft Excel.

5. Click Print.

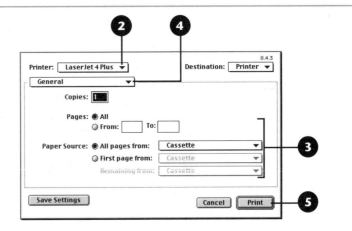

Print Row and Column Titles on Each Page

1 Click the File menu, and click Page Setup.

2 Click the Sheet tab.

3 In the Print Titles area, enter the number of the row or letter of the column letter that contains the titles, or click the appropriate Collapse Dialog button, select the row or column with the mouse, and then click the Expand Dialog button to restore the dialog box.

4 Click OK.

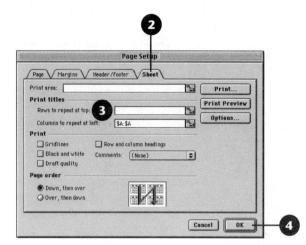

Print Headers and Footers

1 Click the File menu, and click Page Setup.

2 Click the Header/Footer tab.

3 Click Custom Header or Custom Footer.

4 Enter header or footer text, or insert the page number, date, time, filename, or tab name in the Left, Center, or Right section.

5 Click OK.

6 Click OK again.

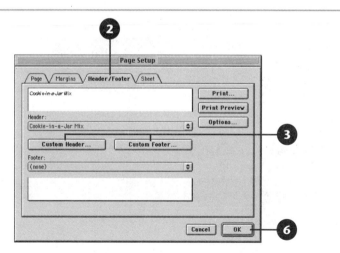

8

Creating a Formula

A *formula* calculates values to return a result. In an Excel worksheet, you use values (such as *147* or *$10.00)*, arithmetic operators (shown in the table), and cell references to create formulas. An Excel formula always begins with the equal sign (=). Although the formulas in the worksheet cells don't display, by default, you can change the view of the worksheet to display them. You can edit formulas just as you do other cell contents, using the formula bar or working in-cell. Using the fill handle, you can quickly copy formulas to adjacent cells.

TIP

Select a cell to enter its address to avoid careless typing mistakes. *Click a cell to insert its cell reference in a formula rather than typing its address.*

Enter a Formula

(1) Click a cell where you want to enter a formula.

(2) Type = (an equal sign) to begin the formula. If you do not begin a formula with an equal sign, Excel will display the information you type; it will not calculate it.

(3) Enter the first argument. An *argument* can be a number or a cell reference. If it is a cell reference, you can type the reference or click the cell in the worksheet.

(4) Enter an arithmetic operator.

(5) Enter the next argument.

(6) Repeat steps 4 and 5 to add to the formula.

(7) Click the Enter button on the formula bar, or press Enter. Notice that the result of the formula appears in the cell and the formula appears in the formula bar.

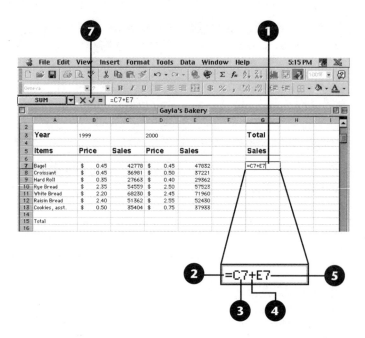

ARITHMETIC OPERATORS		
Symbol	Operation	Example
+	addition	=E3+F3
-	subtraction	=E3-F3
*	multiplication	=E3*F3
/	division	=E3/F3

SEE ALSO

See "Using AutoCalculate and AutoFill" on page 144 for information on automatically filling in a series of numbers, dates, and other items.

TIP

Use the order of precedence to create correct formulas. *Formulas containing more than one arithmetic operator follow the order of precedence. Excel performs its calculations based on the following order: exponentiation, multiplication and division, and finally, addition and subtraction. For example, in the formula 5 + 2 * 3, Excel performs multiplication first (2*3) and addition after (5+6) for a result of 11. To change the order of precedence, use parentheses in a formula— Excel will calculate operations within parentheses first. Using parentheses, the result of (5 + 2) * 3 is 21.*

TIP

What is an absolute cell reference? *When you refer to cell in a formula that doesn't change even if you copy or move it. An absolute cell reference contains a dollar sign ($) to the left of the column or row reference or both.*

Copy a Formula Using the Fill Handle

1 Select the cell that contains the formula you want to copy.

2 Point to the fill handle located in the lower right corner of the selected cell (the pointer changes to a black plus sign).

3 Drag the mouse until the adjacent cells where you want the formula pasted are selected, and then release the mouse button.

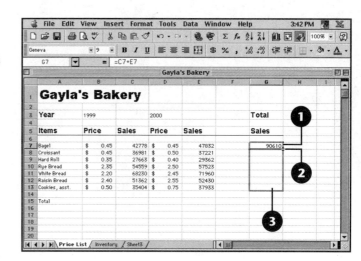

Display Formulas

1 Click the Tools menu, and then click Preferences.

2 Click the View tab.

3 Click to select the Formulas check box.

4 Click OK.

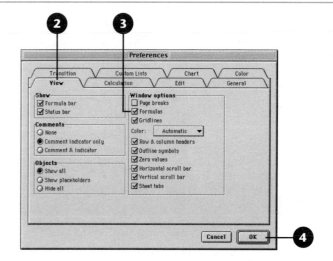

Using Ranges in Formulas

You can simplify formulas by using ranges and range names. For example, if 12 cells in your worksheet contain yearly sales amounts, and you want to multiply each amount by 10%, you can insert one range address in a formula instead of inserting 12 different cell addresses, or you can insert a range name. Using a range name in a formula helps to identify what the formula does; the formula =1997 SALES * .10, for example, is more meaningful than =D7:O7*.10.

Use a Range in a Formula

1 Type an equal sign (=) to begin the formula.

2 Click the first cell of the range, and then drag to select the last cell in the range. Excel enters the range address for you.

3 Complete the formula, and then click the Enter button on the formula bar, or press Enter.

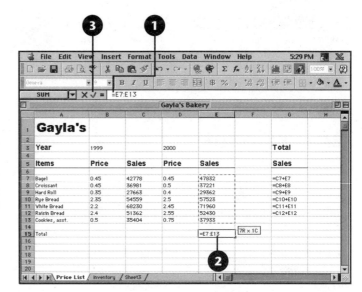

Use a Range Name in a Formula

1 Type an equal sign (=) to begin the formula.

2 Press F3 to display a list of named ranges.

3 Click the name of the range you want to insert.

4 Click OK in the Paste Name dialog box.

5 Complete the formula, and then click the Enter button on the formula bar, or press Enter.

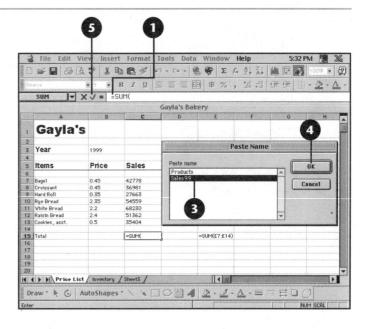

Performing Calculations Using Functions

Functions are predesigned formulas that save you the time and trouble of creating a commonly used equation. Excel includes hundreds of functions that you can use alone or in combination with other formulas or functions. Functions perform a variety of tasks from adding, and averaging to more complicated tasks, such as calculating the monthly payment amount of a loan.

Enter a Function

① Click the cell where you want to enter the function.

② Type = (an equal sign), type the name of the function, and then type (, an opening parenthesis. For example, to insert the SUM function, type =SUM(.

③ Type the argument or click the cell or range you want to insert in the function.

④ Click the Enter button on the formula bar, or press Enter. Excel will automatically add the closing parenthesis to complete the function.

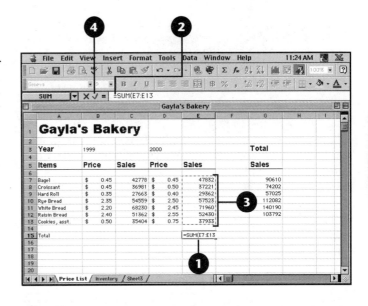

COMMONLY USED EXCEL FUNCTIONS		
Function	**Description**	**Sample**
SUM	Displays the sum of the argument	=SUM(*argument*)
AVERAGE	Displays the average value in the argument	=AVERAGE(*argument*)
COUNT	Calculates the number of values in the argument	=COUNT(*argument*)
MAX	Determines the largest value in the argument	=MAX(*argument*)
MIN	Determines the smallest value in the argument	=MIN(*argument*)
PMT	Determines the monthly payment in a loan	=PMT(*argument*)

Using AutoCalculate and AutoFill

When you want to see the results of a calculation but don't want to insert a formula, you should use AutoCalculate. *AutoCalculate* is a feature that automatically displays the sum, average, maximum, minimum, or count in the status bar of values in whatever cells you select. This result does not appear on the worksheet when printed but is useful for giving you a quick answer while you work. *AutoFill* is a feature that automatically fills in data based on adjacent cells. Using the fill handle, you can enter data in a series, or copy values or formulas to adjacent cells.

SEE ALSO

See "Creating a Formula" on page 140 for information on copying a formula using the fill handle.

Calculate a Range Automatically

1. Select the range of cells you want to calculate. The sum of the selected cells appears in the status bar next to SUM=.

2. If you want to change the type of calculation AutoCalculate performs, Command-click the AutoCalculate display in the status bar.

3. Click the type of calculation you want.

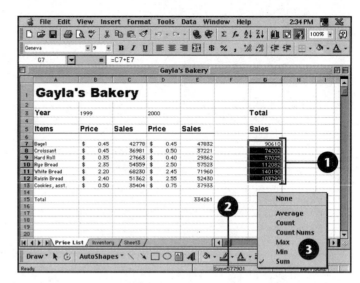

Fill in Data Automatically

1. Select the first cell in the range you want to fill, enter the starting value for the series, and then press Enter.

2. Hold down Control as you drag the fill handle located in the lower right corner of the selected cell (the pointer changes to a black plus sign) over the range.

3. On the shortcut menu, select the type of series you want.

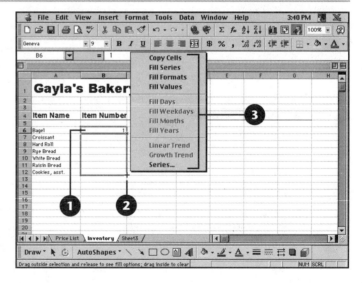

Designing a Worksheet with Excel 98

In addition to using a worksheet to calculate values, you can also use it to manage a list of information, sometimes called a *database*. You can use a Microsoft Excel 98 worksheet to keep an inventory list, a school grade book, or a customer database. Excel provides a variety of tools that make it easy to keep lists up to date and analyze them to get the information you want quickly. For example, you can use these tools to find out how many inventory items are out of stock, which students are earning an A average, or which product is the best selling item.

Analyzing Worksheet Data

Excel's data analysis tools include alphanumeric organizing (called *sorting*), displaying information that meets specific criteria (called *filtering*), and summarizing of data within a table (called a *PivotTable*).

You can analyze data directly in a worksheet, or use a feature called a *Data Form*, an on-screen data entry tool similar to a paper form. A Data Form lets you easily enter data by filling in blank text boxes, and then it adds the information to the bottom of the list. This tool makes entering information in a lengthy list a snap!

Formatting Text and Numbers

You can change the appearance of the data in the cells of a worksheet without changing the actual value in the cell. You can format text and numbers with *font attributes*, such as bolding, italics, or underlining, to enhance this data to catch the reader's eye and to focus the reader's attention. You can also apply *numeric formats* to the numbers in a worksheet to better reflect the type of information they present—dollar amounts, dates, decimals, and so on. For example, you can format a number to display up to 15 decimal places or none at all.

SEE ALSO

See "Selecting Multiple Cells" on page 130 for more information about selecting cells before formatting them.

Format Text Quickly

1. Select a cell or range that contains the text you want to format.

2. Click the Bold, Italic or Underline button on the Formatting toolbar to apply the attribute you want to the selected range. You can also click the Font or Font Size drop-down arrow, and then select a font or font size.

   You can apply more than one attribute as long as the range is selected.

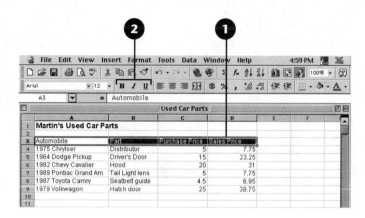

Format Text Using the Format Cells Dialog Box

1. Select a cell or range that contains the text you want to format.

2. Click the Format menu, and then click Cells.

3. Click the Font tab.

4. Click to select the font, font style, and size you want.

5. Select the formatting options you want to apply.

6. Preview your selections.

7. Click OK.

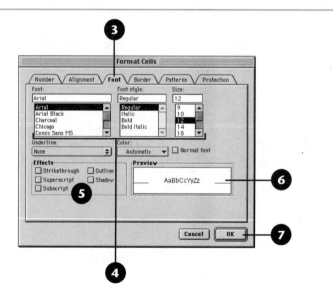

Format Numbers Quickly

1 Select a cell or range that contains the number(s) you want to format.

2 Click the Currency Style, Percent Style, Comma Style, Increase Decimal, or Decrease Decimal button on the Formatting toolbar to apply the numeric attribute you want to the selected range.

You can apply more than one attribute as long as the range is selected.

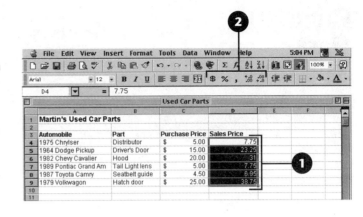

Format Numbers Using the Format Cells Dialog Box

1 Select a cell or range that contains the number(s) you want to format.

2 Click the Format menu, and then click Cells.

3 Click the Number tab.

4 Click to select a category.

5 Select the formatting options you want to apply.

6 Preview your selections.

7 Click OK.

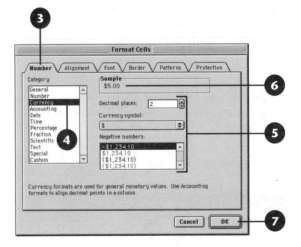

9

Changing Data Alignment

When you enter data in a cell, Excel aligns labels on the left edge of the cell and aligns values and formulas on the right edge of the cell. How Excels aligns the contents of a cell relative to the left or right edge of a cell is known as *horizontal alignment* and how Excel aligns cell contents relative to the top and bottom of a cell is called *vertical alignment*. Excel also provides an option for changing the flow and angle of characters within a cell. The *orientation* of the contents of a cell is expressed in degrees. The default orientation is 0° in which characters appear horizontally within a cell.

TIP

Change simple alignment quickly. *Select a cell or range, and then select the Align Left, Center, or Align Right button on the Formatting toolbar.*

Change Alignment Using the Format Cells Dialog Box

(1) Select a cell or range that contains the data you want to realign.

(2) Click the Format menu, and then click Cells.

(3) Click the Alignment tab.

(4) Click the Horizontal pop-up menu, and then select an alignment.

(5) Click the Vertical pop-up menu, and then select an alignment.

(6) Select an orientation by clicking a point on the orientation map or by clicking the Degrees up or down arrow.

(7) If necessary, click one or more Text Control check boxes.

(8) Click OK.

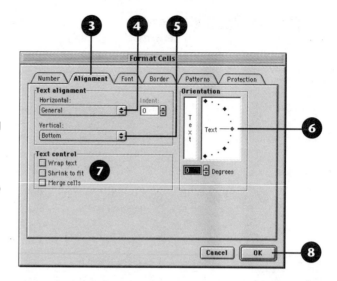

ALIGNMENT TOOLBAR BUTTONS

Icon	Button Name	Description
	Align Left	Aligns cell contents on the left edge of the cell
	Center	Centers the cell contents in the middle of the cell
	Align Right	Aligns cell contents on the right edge of the cell
	Merge And Center	Centers cell contents accross the columns of a selected range

Adding Borders to Cells

You've probably found that the light gray grid that displays on the worksheet screen helps your eyes connect from cell to cell. However, Excel does not include this grid on printouts. You can choose to print gridlines using the Page Setup dialog box or improve on the grid pattern by adding different types of borders to a worksheet. You can add borders to some or all sides of a single cell or range. You can select borders of varying line widths and colors.

TIP

Add a border quickly. *Select a cell or range, click the Borders drop-down arrow on the Formatting toolbar, and then select a border style.*

Apply a Border Using the Format Cells Dialog Box

1 Select a cell or range where you want to apply borders, or to select the entire worksheet, click the Select All button.

2 Click the Format menu, and then click Cells.

3 Click the Border tab.

4 Select a line type from the Style box.

5 If you want a border on the outside of a cell or range, or lines inside a range of cells, click the Outline or Inside icon. If you want to remove a border, click the None icon.

6 To choose the other available Border options, click a Border icon, or click in the Border box at the location where you want the border to appear.

7 Click the Color pop-up menu, and then select a color for the border you have selected.

8 Click OK.

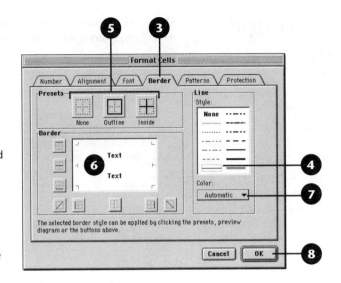

9

Creating a Chart

You have many choices to make when you create a chart, from choosing the chart type you want to use to choosing the objects you want to include and the formatting you want to apply. Excel simplifies the chart-making process with a feature called the Chart Wizard. The *Chart Wizard* is a series of dialog boxes that leads you through all the steps necessary to create an effective chart. You pick and choose from different chart types and styles and select any options you might want to apply while the Chart Wizard is open. Any options you don't add while the Chart Wizard is open can always be added later.

Chart Wizard button

Create a Chart Using the Chart Wizard

1. Select the data range you want to chart. Make sure you include the data you want to chart *and* the column and row labels in the range. The Chart Wizard expects to find this information and automatically incorporates it in your chart.

2. Click the Chart Wizard button on the Standard toolbar.

3. Click a chart type.

4. Click a chart sub-type.

5. Click the Press And Hold To View Sample button to preview your selection.

6. Click Next.

7. Make sure the correct data range is selected.

8. Select the appropriate option button to plot the data series in rows or in columns.

9. Click Next.

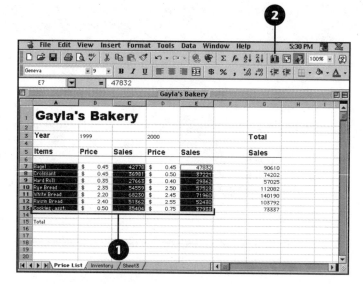

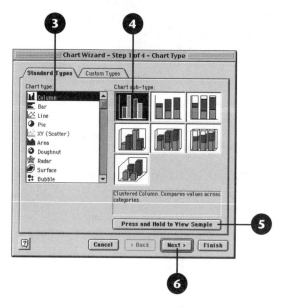

TIP

You can make changes while using the Chart Wizard. *Click the Back button to make changes before clicking the Finish button.*

Place Chart As Object

Place Chart As Sheet

SEE ALSO

See "Inserting a Graph Chart in a Slide" on page 206 for more information about charting.

SEE ALSO

See "Embedding and Linking Information" on page 224 for more information on embedding a chart.

10 To identify the data in the chart, type the titles in the appropriate text boxes.

11 Click Next.

12 Select the option you want to place the chart on a new sheet or on an existing sheet. If you choose to place the chart on an existing sheet rather than on a new sheet, the chart is called an *embedded object*.

13 Click Finish.

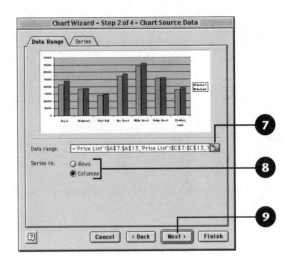

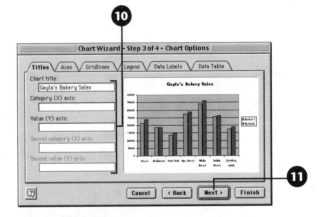

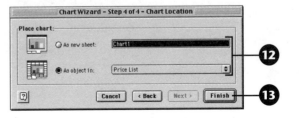

Adding and Deleting a Data Series

Each range of data that comprises a bar, column, or pie slice is called a *data series;* each value in a data series is called a *data point*. The data series is defined when you select a range and then open the Chart Wizard.

But what happens if you want to add a data series once a chart is complete? Using Excel, you can add a data series by changing the data range information in the Chart Wizard, by using the Chart menu, or by dragging a new data series into an existing chart.

As you create and modify more charts, you might also find it necessary to delete one or more data series. You can easily delete a data series by selecting the series and pressing the Delete key.

Add a Data Series to a Chart Quickly

1. Select the range that contains the data series you want to add to your chart.

2. Drag the range into the existing chart, and then release the mouse button.

Excel automatically displays the chart with the added data series.

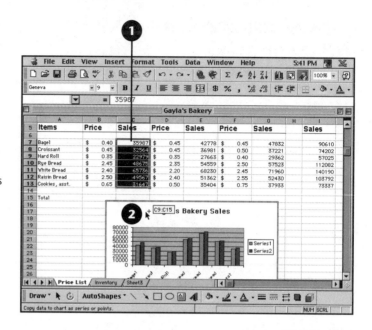

Delete a Data Series

1. Select the chart that contains the data series you want to delete.

2. Click any data point in the data series.

3. Press Delete, and then press Enter.

Excel automatically displays the chart without the deleted data series.

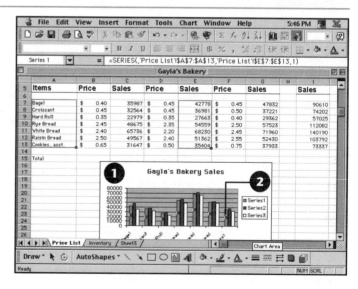

TIP

You can choose to delete one data point in a chart. *To delete one data point but keep the rest of the series in the chart, click the data point twice so that it is the only point selected, and then press the Delete key.*

TIP

Use the Undo button to reverse a deletion. *Click the Undo button on the Standard toolbar to restore the deleted data series or data point to the chart.*

SEE ALSO

See "Enhancing a Chart" on page 154 for more information on how to customize your chart(s) to fit your needs.

TIP

Add a trendline. *A trendline helps you analyze problems of prediction. Select the chart you want to add a trendline, click the Chart menu, click Add Trendline, select a trend type, and then click OK.*

Add a Data Series Using the Add Data Dialog Box

1. Select the chart to which you want to add a data series.

2. Click the Chart menu, and then click Add Data.

3. Click the Collapse Dialog Box button or type the range in the Range box.

4. Drag the pointer over the new range you want to add.

5. Click the Expand Dialog Box button.

6. Click OK.

Change a Data Series

1. Select the chart for which you want to change a data series.

2. Click the Chart menu, and then click Source Data.

3. Click the Series tab.

4. Click the series name you want to change.

5. Click the Collapse Dialog Box button to change the Name or Values.

6. Click OK.

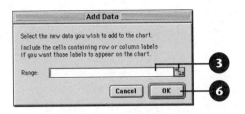

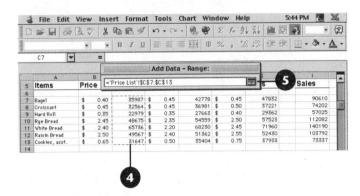

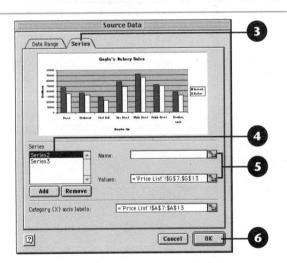

9

Enhancing a Chart

You can add *chart objects,* such as titles, legends, and text annotations, and *chart options,* such as gridlines, to a chart to enhance the appearance of the chart and increase its overall effectiveness. A *chart title* helps to identify the primary purpose of the chart, and a title for each axis further clarifies the data that is plotted. Titles can be more than one line and formatted just like other worksheet text. You can format any element in a chart to add interest. You can change color, patterns, labels, fonts, scale, and alignment. A *legend* helps the reader connect the colors and patterns in a chart with the data they represent. *Gridlines* are horizontal and vertical lines you can add to help the reader determine data point values in a chart that without the gridlines would be difficult to read.

Add a Title

1. Select a chart to which you want to add a title or titles.

2. Click the Chart menu, and then click Chart Options.

3. Click the Titles tab.

4. Type the text you want for the title of the chart.

5. Press Tab and type a title for the x-axis.

6. Press Tab and type a title for the y-axis.

7. Click OK.

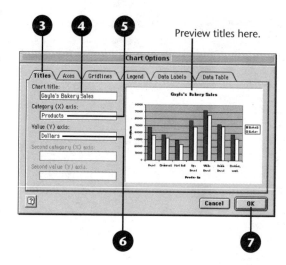

Preview titles here.

Add or Delete a Legend

1. Select the chart to which you want to add or delete a legend.

2. Click the Chart menu, and then click Chart Options.

3. Click the Legend tab.

4. Click the Show Legend check box to add or delete a legend.

5. Click a Placement option to indicate the location of the legend.

6. Click OK.

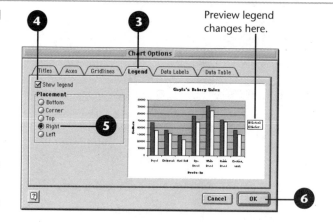

Preview legend changes here.

Format a Chart Element

1. Select a chart to which you want to format an element.

2. Double-click the chart element you want to format.

3. Click the appropriate tab with the type of change you want to make.

4. Click the formatting options you want to change or apply.

5. Click OK.

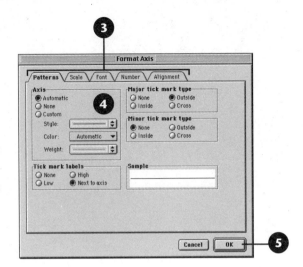

Add Gridlines

1. Select a chart to which you want to add gridlines.

2. Click the Chart menu, and then click Chart Options.

3. Click the Gridlines tab.

4. Select the type of gridlines you want for the x-axis (vertical) and the y-axis (horizontal).

5. Click OK.

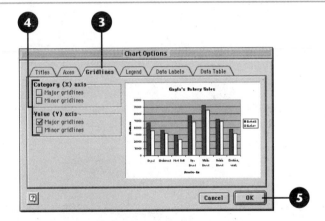

9

Understanding List Terminology

A database is a collection of related records. Examples of databases are an address book, a list of customers or products, and a telephone directory. In Excel, a database is referred to as *list*.

Record
One set of related fields, such as all the fields pertaining to one customer or one product. In a worksheet, each row represents a unique record.

List range
The block of cells that contains the list or part of the list you want to analyze. The list range cannot occupy more than one worksheet.

Field name
The title given to a field. In an Excel list, the first row contains the names of each field. Each field name's maximum length is 255 characters, including upper and lowercase letters and spaces.

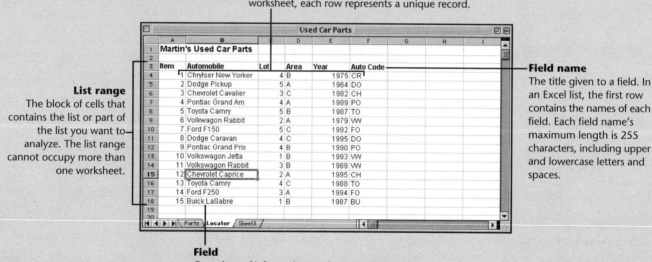

Field
One piece of information, such as customer's last name or an item's code number. In a worksheet, each column represents a field.

Creating a List

To create a list in Excel, you can enter data in worksheet cells, just as you do any other worksheet data, but the placement of the field names and list range must follow these rules:

- ◆ Field names must occupy a single row and be the first row in the list.

- ◆ Enter each record in a single row, with each field in the column corresponding to the field name.

- ◆ Do not include any blank rows within the list range.

- ◆ Do not use more than one worksheet for a list range.

Don't worry about entering records in any particular order; Excel offers several tools for organizing an existing list.

TIP

Create a PickList. *Select the cells with the items you want to include in the PickList, Control-click any cell included in the PickList, and then click Pick From List.*

Create a List

(1) Open a blank worksheet, or use a worksheet that has enough empty columns and rows for the list.

(2) Enter a name for each field in adjacent columns across the first row of the list.

(3) Enter the field information for each record in a separate row, starting with the row directly beneath the field names.

Take advantage of features, such as AutoComplete, that make data entry easier.

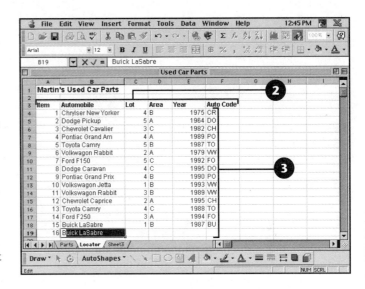

Enter a Label Using the PickList

(1) Control-click the cell where you want to enter a label, and then click Pick From List.

(2) Select an entry from the pop-up menu.

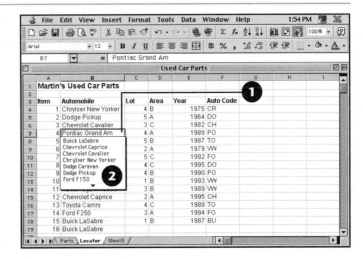

Sorting Data in a List

Once you enter records in a list, you can reorganize the information by filtering or sorting the records. Instead of viewing the entire list, you can use *AutoFilter* to select the part of the list you want to display in the column. Sometimes, you might want to sort records in a client list alphabetically by last name or numerically by date of their last invoice. You can sort a list alphabetically or numerically, in ascending or descending order using a field or fields you choose as the basis for the sort. You can sort a list on one field using the Standard toolbar or on multiple fields using the Data menu. A simple sort—such as organizing a telephone directory alphabetically by last name—can be made complex by adding more than one *sort field* (a field used to sort the list).

Display Parts of a List

1 Click anywhere within the list range.

2 Click the Data menu, point to Filter, and then click AutoFiler.

3 Click the pop-up menu of the field you want to use to specify search criteria.

4 Select the item that records must match in order to be included in the list.

5 Click the Data menu, point to Filter, and then click AutoFiler to redisplay all records in the list.

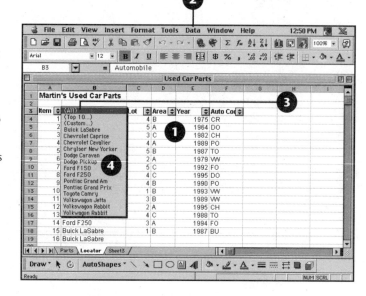

Sort Data Quickly

1 Click a field name you want to sort on.

2 Click the Sort Ascending or the Sort Descending button on the Standard toolbar.

In a list sorted in ascending order, records beginning with a number in the sort field appear first (0-9, A-Z).

In a list sorted in descending order, records beginning with a letter in the sort field appear first (Z-A, 9-0).

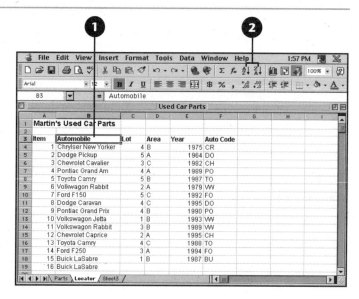

Protect your original list order with an index field. *Before sorting a list for the first time, try to include an index field, a field that contains ascending consecutive numbers (1, 2, 3, etc.). That way, you'll always be able to restore the original order of the list.*

Sort data in rows. *If the data you want to sort is listed across a row instead of down a column, click the Options button in the Sort dialog box, and then click the Sort Left To Right option button in the Sort Options dialog box.*

Sort a List Using More than One Field

1 Click anywhere within the list range.

2 Click the Data menu, and then click Sort.

3 Click the Sort By pop-up menu, and then select the field on which the sort will be based (the *primary sort field*).

4 Click the Ascending or Descending option button.

5 Click the first Then By pop-up menu, select a secondary sort field, and then click the Ascending or Descending option button.

6 If necessary, click the second Then By drop-down arrow, select a tertiary sort field, and then click the Ascending or Descending option button.

7 Click the Header Row option button to *exclude* the field names (in the first row) from the sort, or click the No Header Row option button to *include* the field names (in the first row) in the sort.

8 Click OK.

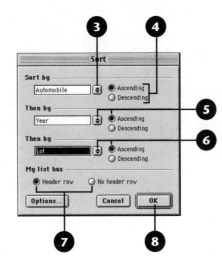

9

Analyzing Data Using a PivotTable

When you want to summarize information in a lengthy list using complex criteria, use the PivotTable to simplify your task. Without the PivotTable, you would have to manually count or create a formula to calculate which records met certain criteria, and then create a table to display that information for a report or presentation. Once you determine what fields and criteria you want to use to summarize the data and how you want the resulting table to look, the PivotTable Wizard does the rest.

TIP

Use the Office Assistant to get help. *Click the Office Assistant button in the lower left corner of the dialog box for help using the PivotTable Wizard.*

Create a PivotTable

1 Click any cell within the list range.

2 Click the Data menu, and then click PivotTable Report.

3 If using the list range, make sure the Microsoft Excel List Or Database option button is selected.

4 Click Next.

5 If the range you want is "Database" (the active list range), then skip to step 8.

6 If the range does not include the correct data, click the Collapse Dialog Box button.

7 Drag the pointer over the list range, including the field names, to select a new range, and then click the Expand Dialog Box button.

8 Click Next.

9 Drag field name(s) to the ROW and COLUMN and DATA areas.

10 Click Next.

11 Specify the location of the worksheet you want to use in the text box, and then click Finish.

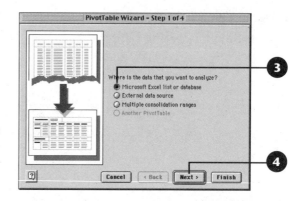

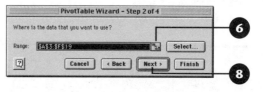

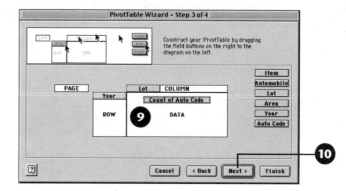

Charting a PivotTable

Data summarized in a PivotTable is an ideal candidate for a chart, since the table itself represents an overwhelming amount of difficult-to-read data. Once you select data within the PivotTable (using buttons on the PivotTable toolbar), then you can chart it like any other worksheet data using the Chart Wizard.

SEE ALSO

See "Creating a Chart" on page 150 for more information about using the Chart Wizard.

Create a Chart from a PivotTable

(1) Click the PivotTable pop-up menu on the PivotTable toolbar, point to Select, and then click Label And Data, or click the Select Label And Data button on the PivotTable toolbar.

(2) Click the Chart Wizard button on the Standard toolbar.

(3) Make your selections in each of the four Chart Wizard dialog boxes.

(4) When you're done, click Finish.

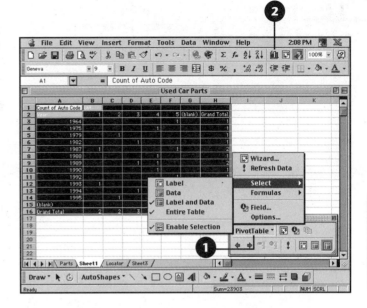

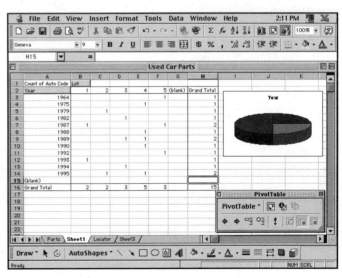

Tracking Changes in a Worksheet

As you build and fine-tune a worksheet, you can keep track of all the changes that are made at each stage in the process. The Track Changes feature makes it easy to know who has made what changes and when the changes were made. To take full advantage of this feature, turn it on the first time you or a co-worker edit a workbook. Then when it's time to review the workbook, all the changes will be recorded. You can review a workbook at any point to see what changes have been made and who made them. Cells containing changes are surrounded by a blue border, and the changes made can be viewed instantly by moving your mouse pointer over any outlined cell. When you're ready to finalize the workbook, you can review it and either accept or reject the changes.

Turn On the Track Changes Feature

1. Click the Tools menu, point to Track Changes, and then click Highlight Changes.

2. Click the Track Changes While Editing check box.

3. Click OK.

4. Click OK to save the workbook and to continue working.

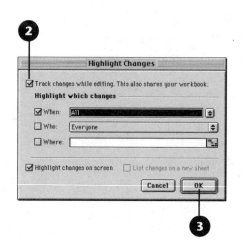

View Changes That Are Tracked

1. Position the mouse pointer over an edited cell (the cell with the triangle in the left corner).

2. To hide the comment, move the mouse pointer away from the edited cell.

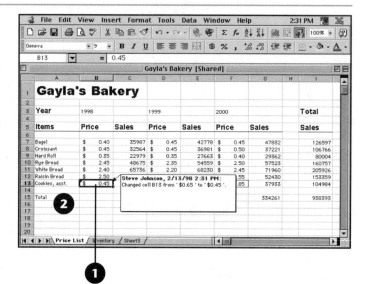

Title bar changes to alert you of shared status. *When you or another user apply the Track Changes command to a workbook, the message "[Shared]" appears in the title bar of the workbook to alert you that this feature is active.*

See "Editing Cell Contents" on page 128 for more information about changing the contents of a cell.

Make your workbook exclusive again. *To remove the shared status, click the Tools menu, point to Track Changes, click Highlight Changes, click to deselect the Track Changes While Editing check box, and then click Yes to make the workbook exclusive.*

Accept or Reject Tracked Changes

(**1**) Click the Tools menu, point to Track Changes, and then click Accept Or Reject Changes.

If necessary, click OK to save the workbook.

(**2**) Click OK to begin reviewing changes.

(**3**) If necessary, scroll to review all the changes, and then click:

◆ Accept to make the selected change to the worksheet.

◆ Reject to remove the selected change from the worksheet.

◆ Accept All to make all the changes to the worksheet after you have reviewed them.

◆ Reject All to remove all the changes to the worksheet after you have reviewed them.

(**4**) Click Close.

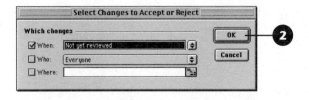

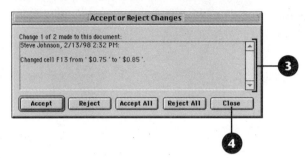

Protecting Your Data

You work very hard creating and entering information in a workbook. To preserve all your work—particularly if your files are being used by others—you can password protect its contents. You can protect a sheet or an entire workbook. In each case, you'll be asked to supply a password, and then enter it again when you want to work on the file.

Protect Your Worksheet

1 Click the Tools menu, point to Protection, and then click Protect Sheet.

Using the Tools menu, you can protect an individual sheet, the entire workbook, or you can protect and share a workbook. The steps for all are similar.

2 Click the check boxes for the options you want protected in the sheet.

3 Type a password.

A password contains any combination of letters, numbers, spaces, and symbols. Excel passwords are case sensitive so you must type upper- and lowercase letters correctly when you set or enter passwords.

4 Click OK.

5 Retype the password.

6 Click OK.

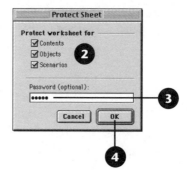

Building Powerful Worksheets with Excel 98

I f your worksheet or workbook needs go beyond simple calculations, Microsoft Excel 98 offers several tools to help you create worksheets that address more specialized projects. With Excel's linking capabilities, you can share data among worksheets and workbooks.

Linking and Sharing Data in Excel

For many projects, you might need to use more than one worksheet to record, analyze, or present information. If you run a business, for example, you might use one Excel worksheet to maintain a price list for your products or services and another worksheet as an invoice form. When you generate an invoice, you need to enter the price for each product. You could check the price list and then enter the price for each product purchased. But what if your prices change often? You'd have to look up each price and enter it every time you generate an invoice. A better solution is to establish a link. You can link a formula that references a cell in the price list worksheet to a cell in the invoice worksheet, so that the invoice worksheet always reflects the most up-to-date prices. Linking makes it easy to calculate results no matter how often your worksheet changes, because it automatically updates values as necessary.

Customizing Excel

To create a work environment that addresses your needs, Excel offers a variety of options that can be customized. The Preferences dialog box contains tabs for changing General options, such as the default font and the number of sheets in a new workbook, Edit options, such as where to move the active cell after you enter data and whether to allow drag-and-drop cell moving, Calculation options, such as whether you want Excel to automatically recalculate a worksheet whenever you change a value, and many more aspects of working in the program.

TIP

Change cell selection after you press the Enter key. *On the Edit tab, click the Direction pop-up menu, and then select a direction to change the direction of the cell pointer after you press the Enter key.*

Change General Options

(1) Click the Tools menu, and then click Preferences.

(2) Click the General tab.

(3) To turn on a setting in Excel, click the check box for the option you want.

(4) To change the number of recently used files listed at the bottom of the File menu, click the spin arrows to set the number of files you want.

(5) To change the default number of sheets in a new workbook, click the spin arrows to set a number.

(6) To change the default font, click the Standard Font pop-up menu, and then select a new font.

(7) To change the default font size, click the Size pop-up menu, and then select a new font size.

(8) To specify where Excel should automatically look for existing files or newly saved files, enter the location of your default folder.

(9) Click the User Name text box and edit its contents.

(10) Click OK.

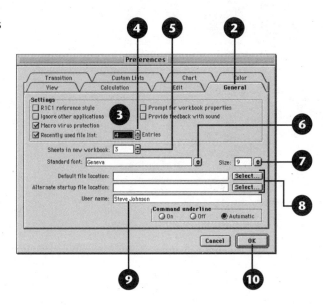

Freezing Columns and Rows

Large worksheets present a particular dilemma when it comes to working efficiently. If you scroll down to see the bottom of the list, you can no longer see the column names at the top of the list. Instead of repeatedly scrolling up and down, you can temporarily fix, or *freeze*, those column or row headings so that you can see them no matter where you scroll in the worksheet.

When you freeze a row or column, you are actually splitting the screen into one or more *panes* (window sections) and freezing one of the panes. You can split the screen into up to four panes and can freeze up to two of these panes. You can edit the data in a frozen pane just as you do any Excel data, but the cells remain stationary even when you use the scroll bars; only the unfrozen part(s) of the screen scrolls.

Freeze Columns and Rows

1 Click any cell in the row below the rows you want to freeze, or in the column to the right of the columns you want to freeze.

2 Click the Window menu, and then click Freeze Panes.

◆ When you freeze a pane horizontally, all the rows *above* the active cell freeze. When you freeze a pane vertically, all the columns to the *left* of the active cell freeze.

◆ When you freeze a pane, it has no effect on how a worksheet looks when printed.

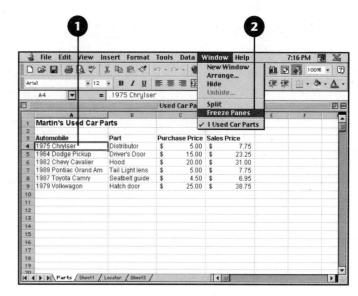

Unfreeze Columns and Rows

1 Click the Window menu, and then click Unfreeze Panes.

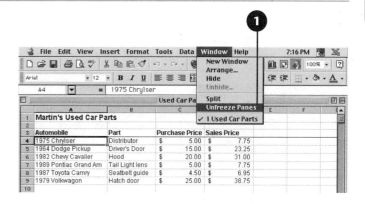

Adding Records Using a Data Form

A *Data Form* is an optional method of entering information in a list range. Once field names are entered, you access a Data Form using the Data menu. You don't even need to select the list range first; as long as the active cell is somewhere within the list range when the Data Form is opened, Excel will automatically locate the list.

As you add new records to the form, the list range is constantly updated to include the new rows. This means that as new records are added, Excel automatically enlarges the list range.

> **TIP**
>
> **Use wildcards to find data in a list quickly.** *The wildcard "?" stands for any single character, while "*" stands for many characters. R?N might find RAN or RUN while R*N might find RUN, RAN, RUIN, or RATION.*

Add Records Using a Data Form

(1) Click any cell within the list range.

(2) Click the Data menu, and then click Form.

(3) Click New.

(4) Type each field entry in the appropriate text box. Move from field to field by pressing the Tab key or by clicking in each field.

(5) Click Close.

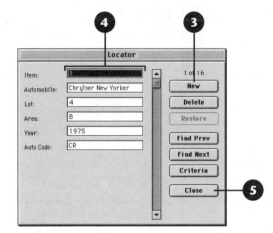

Delete a Record

(1) Click anywhere within the list range.

(2) Click the Data menu, and then click Form.

(3) Click Find Prev or Find Next to advance to the record you want to delete.

(4) Click Delete

(5) Click OK to confirm the deletion.

(6) Click Close.

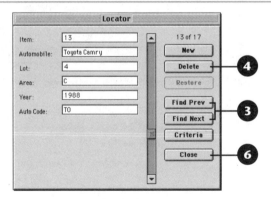

Managing Records Using a Data Form

You can use a Data Form to display, edit, or delete selected records within a list. To display only selected records in the Data Form, you specify the search *criteria*—the information a record must contain—in the Data Form, and Excel uses that criteria to find and display matching records. Although the Data Form only shows the records that match your criteria, the other records still exist in the list. If more than one record matches your criteria, you can use the Data Form buttons to move through the records, editing or deleting them.

TIP

You can return to the complete list of records at any time. *Return to the initial Data Form by clicking the Form button in the Locator dialog box.*

Display Selected Records

1. Click anywhere within the list range.

2. Click the Data menu, and then click Form.

3. Click Criteria.

4. Type the information you want matching records to contain. You can fill in one or more fields.

5. Click Find Prev or Find Next to advance to a matching record.

6. Click Close.

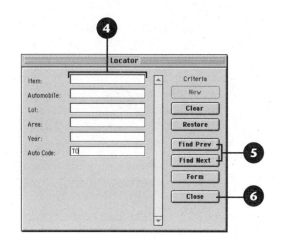

Edit a Record

1. Click anywhere within the list range.

2. Click the Data menu, and then click Form.

3. Find a record that requires modification.

4. Click in the field you want to edit to position the insertion point, and then use the Delete or Del key to modify the text.

5. Click Close.

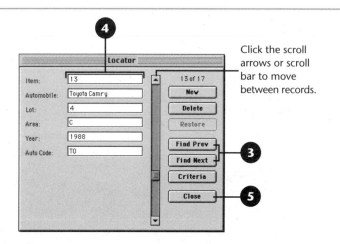

Click the scroll arrows or scroll bar to move between records.

Working with Templates

You may not realize it, but every workbook you create is based on a template. When you start a new workbook without specifying a template, Excel creates a new workbook based on the *default template*, which includes three work-sheets and no special formulas, labels, or formatting. When you specify a particular template in the New dialog box, whether it's one supplied by Excel or one you created yourself, Excel starts a new workbook that contains the formulas, labels, graphics, and formatting contained in that template. The template itself does not change when you enter data in the new work-book, because you are working on a new file, not with the template file. If you want to make changes to the template form itself, so that all new workbooks are based on its change, you need to open the template and make your changes there.

Open a Template

1. Click the Open button on the Standard toolbar.

2. Click the pop-up menu, and then select the drive and folder that contains the template you want to open.

3. Click the List Files Of Type pop-up menu, and then select Templates.

4. Click the filename of the template you want open.

5. Click Open.

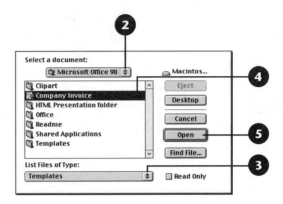

Create a New Template

1. Enter all the information you want in a new workbook—including formulas, labels, graphics, and formatting.

2. Click the File menu, and then click Save As.

3. Click the pop-up menu, and then select a location for the template.

4. Type a filename that will help you easily identify the template.

5. Click the Save File As Type pop-up menu, and then select Templates.

6. Click Save.

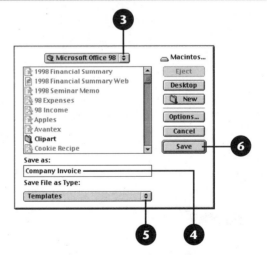

TIP

Use the New Workbook button to open a default workbook. *Clicking the New Workbook button on the Standard toolbar opens a workbook based on the default template.*

TIP

Changing the default template affects all new workbooks you create. *Be careful if you decide to make any changes to this template.*

TIP

Test your template as you work. *As you build a template, enter data in it to make sure the formulas work correctly. Then before saving it as a template, erase the data.*

TIP

When to use macros and templates. *Create a macro to make repetitive tasks more efficient; create a template for fill-in-the-blank data whose format rarely changes.*

Customize an Excel Template

1 Open the Excel template you want to customize. Excel templates are located in the Templates folder within the Microsoft Office 98 folder.

2 Click the Customize Your [Template Name] tab.

3 Point to cell notes for comments that help you customize the template.

4 Replace the placeholder text with your own information.

5 Make any final changes you want. Remember that these changes will affect all new workbooks you create using this template.

6 Click the Save button on the Standard toolbar.

7 Close the template before using it to create a new workbook.

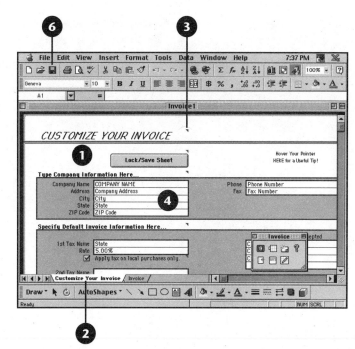

10

Sharing Workbooks

When you're working with others on a network, you often want to enable them to share workbooks you have created, as well as the responsibilities of entering and maintaining the data in them. *Sharing* means users can add columns and rows, enter data, and change formatting, but allows you to review their changes. This type of work arrangement is particularly effective in a team situation in which many users have responsibilities for different types of data—all of which are included in the same workbook. Once a workbook is stored on a network, you can take advantage of tools enabling multiple users to share a single file. In cases in which the same cells are modified by multiple users, Excel can keep track of changes, and you can accept or reject them at a later date.

Enable Workbook Sharing

(**1**) Open the workbook(s) you want to share.

(**2**) Click the Tools menu, and then click Share Work-book.

(**3**) Click the Editing tab.

(**4**) Click the Allow Changes By More Than One User At The Same Time check box.

(**5**) Click OK and then click OK again to save your workbook.

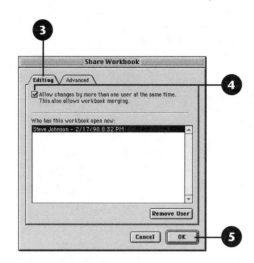

Change Sharing Options

(**1**) Open the workbook(s) you want to share.

(**2**) Click the Tools menu, and then click Share Workbook.

(**3**) Click the Advanced tab, if necessary.

◆ Changes made in a shared workbook can be discarded immediately or kept for any number of days using the Day spin boxes.

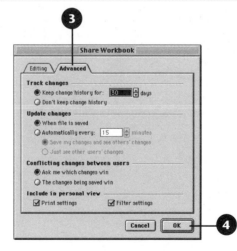

Excel alerts you if you are working in a shared file.
When sharing is enabled, "[Shared]" appears in the title bar of the shared workbook.

See "Viewing the Excel Window" on page 124 for information about arranging worksheets.

See "Freezing Columns and Rows" on page 167 for information about seeing the column or row names at the top or side of the worksheet.

◆ All changes can be saved only when the workbook is saved, or in any combination of your changes and others, in a time interval you specify.

◆ When conflicting changes are made, you can choose to automatically have the last change saved (The Changes Being Saved Win option), or you can be asked by Excel which changes you want to keep (Ask Me Which Changes Win option).

◆ You can choose to save none, either, or both of the personal view settings. Depending on which options are chosen, these are saved with your copy of the shared workbook.

(4) Click OK.

Indicates that the workbook is shared

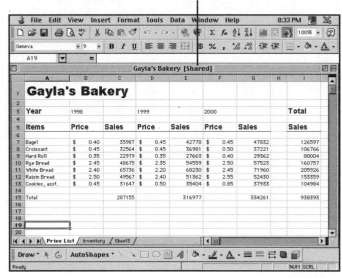

Consolidating Data

In some cases, you'll want to consolidate data from different worksheets or workbooks into a workbook rather than simply linking the source data. For instance, each division in your company is creating a budget, and your task is to pull together the totals for each line item into one company-wide budget. If each divisional budget is laid out in the same way, with the budgeted amount for each line item at the same cell address, you can very easily consolidate all the information without any retyping. And, if data in individual workbooks changes, the consolidated worksheet or workbook will always be correct.

SEE ALSO

See "Creating Links Between Worksheets" on page 176 for information on creating and breaking links.

Consolidate Data from Other Worksheets or Workbooks

1. Open all the workbooks that contain the data you want to consolidate.

2. Open or create the workbook that will contain the consolidated data.

3. Select the destination range. Make sure you select enough cells to accommodate any labels that might be included in the data you are consolidating.

4. Click the Data menu, and then click Consolidate.

5. Click the Function pop-up menu, and then select the function you want to use to consolidate the data.

6. Click the Reference Collapse Dialog Box button and then select the cells to be consolidated, or type the location of the data to be consolidated.

If necessary, use the Window menu to move between workbooks or to arrange them so they are visible at the same time.

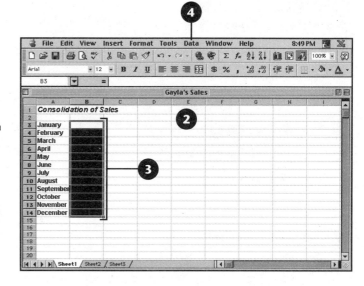

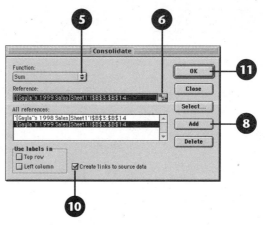

7 Click the Expand Dialog Box button.

8 Click the Add button to add the reference to the list of consolidated ranges.

9 Repeat steps 6 through 8 until you have listed all references to consolidate.

10 Click the Create Links To Source Data check box.

11 Click OK.

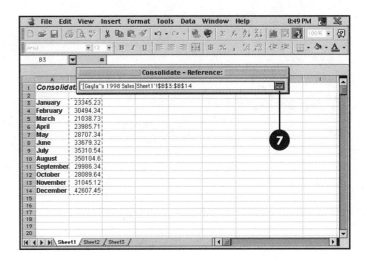

Click the Plus button to see consolidated data.

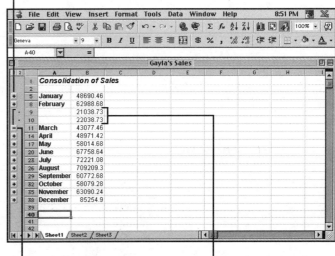

The Minus button indicates consolidated data is displayed.

Consolidate data for March

Creating Links Between Worksheets

A *link* can be as simple as a reference to a cell in another worksheet, or it can be part of a formula. You can link cells between sheets within one workbook or between different workbooks. The data in the cell that you want to link is called the *source data*. The cell or range to which you want to link the source data is called the *destination cell* or *destination range*. If you determine that linked data should no longer be continually updated, you can break a link easily.

TIP

Copy cells when you don't want the data to change.
If you want to use data from another worksheet or workbook but do not want the data to change, simply copy or move the cells by dragging them or using the Clipboard.

Create a Link Between Worksheets

1. Select the destination cell or destination range.

2. Click the Edit Formula button on the formula bar.

3. Click the sheet tab that contains the source data.

4. Select the cell or range that contains the source data.

5. Click OK or click the Enter button on the formula bar.

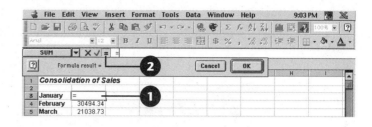

Sheet name indicates that the cell is on a different sheet

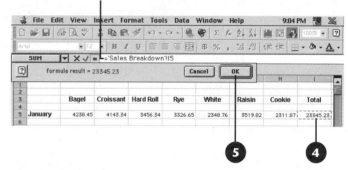

Break a Link

1. Click the cell containing the linked formula you want to break.

2. Click the Copy button on the Standard toolbar.

3. Click the Edit menu, and then click Paste Special.

4. Click the Values option button.

5. Click OK.

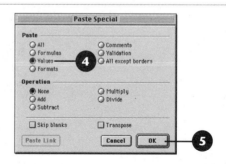

Auditing a Worksheet

When you create formulas on a worksheet, Excel can give visual cues to the relationship between cells in the formula. With the Auditing toolbar, you can examine the relationship between cells and formulas on your worksheet and identify errors. When you use the auditing tools, tracer arrows point out cells that provide data to formulas and the cells that contain formulas that refer to the cells. A box is drawn around ranges of cells that provide data to formulas.

TIP

Circle invalid data. *To circle invalid data in a formula, click the Circle Invalid Data button on the Auditing toolbar. Click the Clear Validation Circles button to clear the circles.*

Audit Cells in a Worksheet

1. Click the cell for which you want to audit.

2. Click the Tools menu, point to Auditing, and then click Show Auditing Toolbar.

3. To find cells that provide data to a formula, select the cell that contains the formula, and then click the Trace Precedents button.

4. To find out which formulas refer to a cell, select the cell and then click the Trace Dependents button.

5. If a formula displays an error value, such as #DIV/0!, click the Trace Error button to locate the problem.

6. To remove arrows, click the Remove Precedent Arrows button, Remove Dependent Arrows button, or Remove All Arrows button.

7. Click the Close box on the Auditing toolbar.

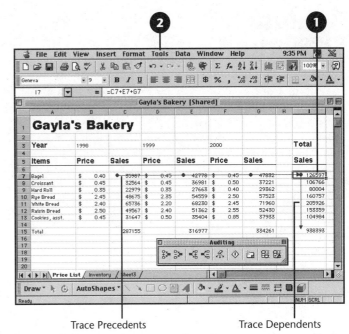

Trace Precedents   Trace Dependents

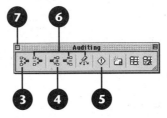

10

Creating Scenarios

Since some worksheet data is constantly evolving, Excel gives you the ability to create multiple sets of values using *scenarios*, which let you speculate on a variety of outcomes. For example, the marketing department might want to see how their budget would be affected if sales decreased by 25%. The ability to create, save, and modify scenarios means a business will be better prepared for different outcomes to avoid economic surprises.

TIP

Don't forget to save your original scenario. *Creating a scenario that contains unchanged values means you'll always be able to return to your original values.*

TIP

Create a custom view. *Modify the display you want to save, click the View menu, click Custom Views, click Add, type a name for the custom view, and then click OK.*

Create and Show a Scenario

1. Click the Tools menu, and then click Scenarios.

2. Click Add.

3. Type a name in the Scenario Name box.

4. Type the cells included in the scenario, or click the Collapse Dialog Box button, use your mouse to select the cells, and then click the Expand Dialog Box button.

5. Type optional comments in the Comment box.

6. Click OK.

7. Type values for each of the displayed changing cells.

8. Click OK.

9. Click Show.

10. Click Summary and then click OK.

11. Click Close.

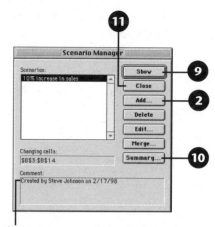

Each time a scenario is edited, Excel automatically adds a comment with the new modification date.

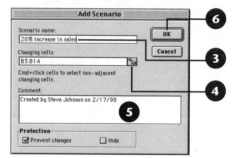

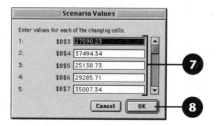

Generating Reports

The sheets, custom views, and scenarios that you create within a workbook combine to produce powerful individual worksheets. Since a workbook contains sheets with related data, you might want to generate reports that contain any combination of the data from your worksheets. Using Excel's Report Manager, you can create reports that contain workbook sheets, as well as custom views and scenarios. You can save and name your reports so you can use them in the future.

TIP

The Report Manager might not be installed. *If you don't see the Report Manager on the View menu, you'll need to install it by running the Value Pack Installer from the Microsoft Office 98 CD.*

Create a Report

1. Open the workbook you want to use to create the report.

2. Create the custom views and the scenarios you want.

3. Click the View menu, and then click Report Manager.

4. Click Add.

5. Type a report name.

6. Click the Sheet pop-up menu, and then select a sheet to add to the report.

7. If necessary, click the View and Scenario pop-up menu to select a view and scenario.

8. Click Add. (Repeat steps 6 through 8 until all the necessary sheets have been added.)

9. To change the order of a section, click the section you want to move, and then click the Move Up or Move Down button.

10. Click OK.

11. To print the report, click Print.

12. Click Close.

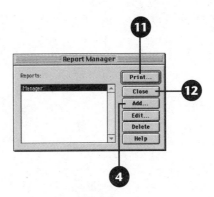

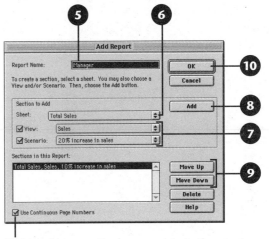

Click to add consecutive page numbers to the report

10

Understanding How Macros Automate Your Work

To complete many tasks in Excel, you need to execute a series of commands and actions. To print two copies of a selected range of Sheet2 of a worksheet, for example, you need to open the workbook, switch to Sheet2, select the print area, open the Print dialog box, and specify that you want to print two copies. If you often need to complete the same task, you'll find yourself repeatedly taking the same series of steps. It can become tiresome and irritating to continually repeat these same commands and actions when you can easily create a mini-program, or *macro*, that accomplishes all of them with a single command.

Creating a macro is easy and requires no programming on your part. Excel simply records the steps you want included in the macro while you use the keyboard and mouse. When you record a macro, Excel stores the list of commands with the name of your choice. You can store your macros in the current workbook, in a new workbook, or in Excel's Personal Macro workbook. Storing your macros in the Personal Macro workbook make the macros available to you from any location in Excel, even when no workbook is open.

Once a macro is created, you can make modifications to it, add comments so other users will understand its purpose, and find out if it runs correctly or not.

You can run a macro by choosing the Macro command on the Tools menu or by using a shortcut key or clicking a toolbar button you've assigned to it. When you click the Tools menu, point to Macro, and then click Macros, the Macro dialog box opens.

From the Macro dialog box, you can create, edit, delete, or run a macro. If you have problems with a macro, you can step through the macro one command at a time, known as *debugging*.

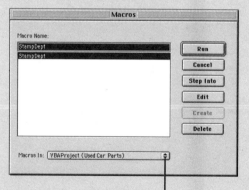

Indicates where the macro is stored

Recording a Macro

Recording a macro is almost as easy as using a tape recorder. Once you turn on the macro recorder, Excel records every mouse click and keystroke action you execute until you turn off the recorder. Then you can "play," or run, the macro whenever you want to repeat that series of actions. You don't even need to press a rewind button!

TRY THIS

Record a macro. *Create a macro that records your name in a cell and includes attractive formatting.*

SEE ALSO

See "Understanding How Macros Automate Your Work" on page 180 for more information on where to save a macro.

Record a Macro

1. Click the Tools menu, point to Macro, and then click Record New Macro.

2. Type a name for the macro. This macro name appears in the list of available macros when you want to run a macro.

3. Assign a shortcut key to use a keystroke combination instead of a menu selection to run the macro.

4. Click the Store Macro In pop-up menu, and then select a location. If you want the macro to be available for all your worksheet, save it in the Personal Macro workbook.

5. Type a description, if you want. The description appears at the bottom of the Macro dialog box.

6. Click OK.

7. Execute each command or action you need to complete the macro's task. Take the time to complete each action correctly, since the macro will repeat all moves you make, but at a much faster rate.

8. Click the Stop Recording button.

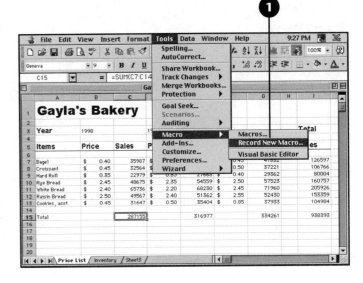

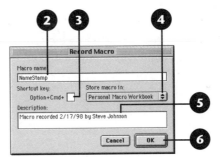

10

Running a Macro

Running a macro is similar to choosing a command in Excel. You can run a macro by selecting a menu command, issuing a keyboard combination, or clicking a toolbar button, just as you might execute any Excel command.

When you record a macro, you can specify how you want to be able to play it back when you need it. You can also assign a toolbar button to a macro. Where you store a macro when you save it determines its availability later. Macros stored in the Excel Personal Macro workbook are always available, and macros stored in any other workbooks are only available when the workbook is open.

TIP

Run a macro. *Click the button assigned to the macro or issue the shortcut key you assigned to the macro.*

Run a Macro Using a Menu Command

(1) Click the Tools menu, point to Macro, and then click Macros.

(2) If necessary, click the Macros In pop-up menu, and then select the workbook that contains the macro you want to run.

(3) Click the name of the macro you want to run.

(4) Click Run.

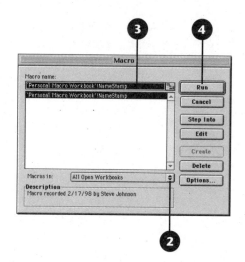

Creating a Presentation with PowerPoint 98

Whether you need to put together a quick presentation of sales figures for your management team or create a polished slide show for your company's stockholders, Microsoft PowerPoint 98 can help you present your information efficiently and professionally.

Introducing PowerPoint

PowerPoint is a *presentation graphics program*: software that helps you create a slide show presentation. PowerPoint makes it easy to generate and organize ideas. It provides tools you can use to create the objects that make up an effective slide show—charts, graphs, bulleted lists, eye-catching text, multimedia video and sound clips, and more. PowerPoint also makes it easy to create slide show supplements, such as handouts, speaker's notes, and transparencies.

When you're ready, you can share your presentation with others, regardless of whether they have installed PowerPoint, in the office or on the Internet, where you can take instant advantage of the power of the World Wide Web from your planning stages right up to showing your presentation. PowerPoint also includes powerful slide show management tools that give you complete control.

Creating a New Presentation

When you first start PowerPoint, a dialog box opens that provides several presentation type options; the option you choose depends on the requirements of your presentation. You can click the Cancel button to close the dialog box without making a selection. You can also create a new presentation once PowerPoint has started by using the File menu.

TIP

You can have more than one presentation open at a time. *This is an especially useful feature when you want to copy slides from one presentation into another. To switch between open presentations, click the Window menu, and then click the presentation you want to switch to.*

Start a New Presentation

1. Start PowerPoint.

2. Click the option button you want to use to begin your presentation.

3. Click OK.

4. Follow the instructions that appear. These will vary, depending on the presentation type you chose.

Helps you generate presentation content

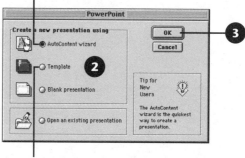

Opens a list of templates, or visual slide designs, from which you preview and then select the icon representing the design you want

Start a New Presentation Within PowerPoint

1. Click the File menu, and then click New.

2. Click the tab to display the options you want to use to begin your presentation.

3. Click the icon you want to use as the basis of your presentation.

4. Click OK.

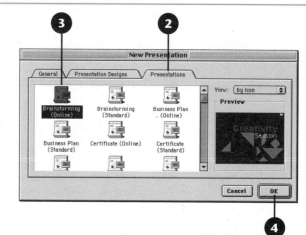

Generating Ideas Using AutoContent Wizard

Often the most difficult part of creating a presentation is knowing where to start. PowerPoint's AutoContent Wizard can help you develop presentation content on a variety of business and personal topics. An AutoContent presentation usually contains 5-10 slides that follow an organized progression of ideas. You edit the text as necessary to meet your needs. Many of the AutoContent presentations are available in Standard and Online Web formats.

TIP

You can use the AutoContent Wizard from the File menu. *Anytime during a PowerPoint session, click the File menu, click New, click the Presentations tab, click the AutoContent Wizard icon, and then click OK.*

Generate a Presentation Using the AutoContent Wizard

1. Start PowerPoint, click the AutoContent Wizard option button in the PowerPoint dialog box, and then click OK.

2. Read the first wizard dialog box, and then click Next.

3. Click the presentation type you want to use; or to focus on just one set of presentations, click the category button you want, and then click the presentation you want.

4. Click Next.

5. Choose the applicable presentation output, and then click Next.

6. Click the presentation style option button you want to use, and then click Next.

7. Enter information for your title slide, and then click Next.

8. Read the last wizard dialog box, and then click Finish.

Category option buttons

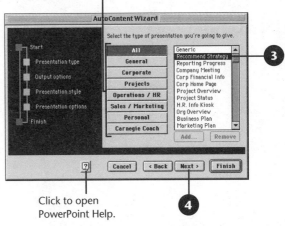

Click to open PowerPoint Help.

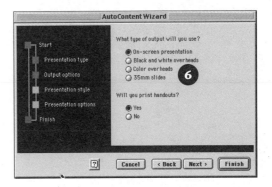

11

Choosing a Template Design

PowerPoint provides a collection of professionally designed templates, which you can use to create effective presentations. Each *template* provides a format and color scheme to which you need only add text. You can choose a new template for your presentation at any point: when you first start your presentation or after you've developed the content.

Apply Design button

TIP

Use a template to create a new presentation. *To create a new presentation with a template, click the File menu, click New, click the Presentation Designs tab, click the presentation design you want to use, and then click OK.*

Create a Presentation with a Template

1. Start PowerPoint, click the Template option button in the PowerPoint dialog box, and then click OK.

2. Click the Presentation Designs tab.

3. Click a presentation design icon you want to use.

4. Click OK.

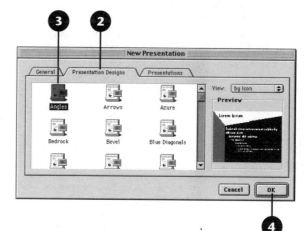

Apply a Template to an Existing Presentation

1. Open the presentation to which you want to apply a template.

2. Click the Apply Design button on the Standard toolbar.

3. Click the template you want to apply to your slides.

4. Click Apply.

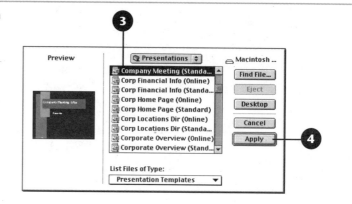

Viewing the PowerPoint Window

The *menu bar* contains the names of the PowerPoint menus that are available. The menus change depending on the task at hand.

The *title bar* displays the presentation name.

The *presentation window* displays the presentation you are currently working on. It has its own Close box in the upper left corner of the window.

The *toolbars* contain buttons you click to carry out commands you use most frequently. You can display toolbars as you need them.

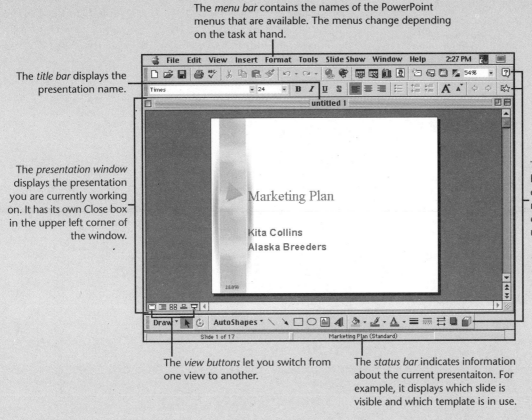

The *view buttons* let you switch from one view to another.

The *status bar* indicates information about the current presentaiton. For example, it displays which slide is visible and which template is in use.

11

The PowerPoint Views

To help you during all aspects of developing a presentation, PowerPoint provides five different views: Slide, Outline, Slide Sorter, Notes Page, and Slide Show. You can switch from one view to another with a single click of one of the view buttons, located to the left of the horizontal scroll bar.

Slide View

Slide view displays one slide at a time. Use this view to modify individual slides. You can move easily through your slides using the scroll bars or the Previous and Next Slide buttons located at the bottom of the vertical scroll bar. When you drag the scroll box up or down the vertical scroll bar, a label appears that indicates which slide will appear if you release the mouse button.

Slide view

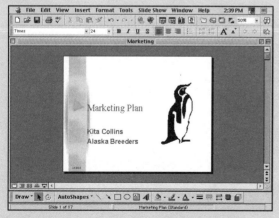

Outline View

Outline view displays a list of the slide titles and their contents in outline format. Use this view to develop your presentation's content. In Outline view, a special toolbar appears that helps you organize and enter your outline. A "thumbnail" or miniature of the active slide appears in a corner to give you an idea of its appearance. Individual slides are numbered. A slide icon appears for each slide. Icons for slides featuring shapes or pictures have small graphics on them.

Outline view

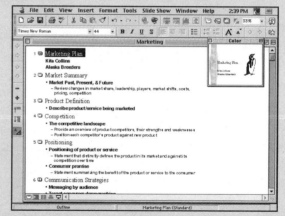

Slide Sorter View

Slide Sorter view displays a thumbnail of each slide in the same window, in the order in which the slides appear in your presentation. Use this view to organize your slides, add

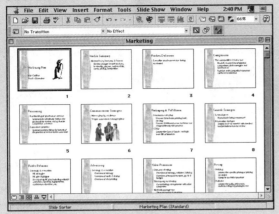

actions between slides, called *slide transitions,* and other effects to your slide show. In Slide Sorter view, a special toolbar appears that helps you add slide transitions and control other aspects of your presentation. When you add a slide transition, a small icon appears that indicates an action will take place as one slide replaces the previous slide during a show. If you hide a slide, a small icon appears that indicates the slide will not show during the presentation.

Notes Page View

Notes Page view displays a reduced view of a single slide along with a large text box in which you can type notes. You can use these notes as you give your presentation. When you work in Notes Page view you will probably need to use the Zoom drop-down arrow to increase the magnification so you can type more easily. Click the Zoom drop-down arrow, and then click the magnification you want.

Slide Show View

Slide Show view presents your slides, one slide at a time. Use this view when you're ready to give your presentation. In Slide Show view, you can click the screen repeatedly or press Return to move through the show until you've shown all the slides. You can exit Slide Show view at any time by pressing Esc. You'll return to the previous view.

11

Creating Consistent Slides

For a presentation to be understandable, the objects on its slides need to be arranged in a visually meaningful way. PowerPoint's *AutoLayout* feature helps you arrange objects on your slide in a consistent manner. There are 24 AutoLayouts that are designed to accommodate the most common slide arrangements. When you create a new slide, you apply an AutoLayout to the slide. Placeholders for text or objects on the AutoLayout appear automatically. You can also apply an AutoLayout to an existing slide at any time.

Insert New Slide button

Insert a New Slide

(1) Click the Insert New Slide button on the Standard toolbar.

(2) Click the AutoLayout that provides the layout you need.

(3) Click OK.

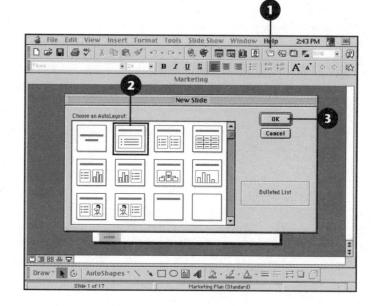

Apply an AutoLayout to an Existing Slide

(1) In Slide view, display the slide you want to change.

(2) Click the Slide Layout button on the Standard toolbar.

(3) Click the AutoLayout you want.

(4) Click Apply.

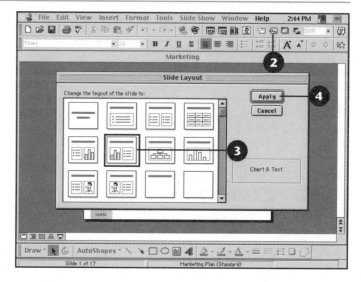

Use AutoLayout to create placeholders. *When you apply an AutoLayout to a slide, an arranged group of placeholders appears—one placeholder for each object on the slide. The placeholders include include instructions for entering object contents.*

Insert slides from other presentations. *In Slide view, display the slide you want to insert the slides after, click the Insert menu, click Slides From File, and then double-click the file you want to insert.*

Delete a slide. *In Slide view, display the slide you want to delete, click the Edit menu, and then click Delete Slide.*

Enter Information into a Placeholder

(1) For text placeholders, click the placeholder and type the necessary text.

For other objects, double-click the placeholder and work with whatever accessory PowerPoint starts.

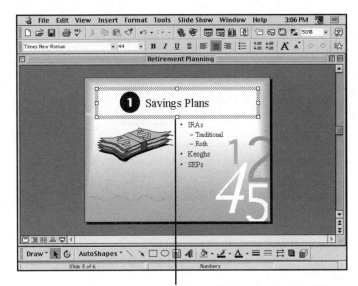

A placeholder is a border that defines the size and location of an object.

AUTOLAYOUT PLACEHOLDERS

Placeholder	Description
Bulleted List	Displays a short list of related points
Clip Art	Inserts a picture
Chart	Inserts a chart
Organization Chart	Insert an organizational chart
Table	Inserts a table from Microsoft Word
Media Clip	Inserts a music, sound, or video clip
Object	Inserts an object created in another program, such as an Excel spreadsheet or WordArt object

11

Entering Text

In Slide view, you type text directly into the text placeholders. If you type more text than fits in the placeholder, you might need to adjust the font size of the text you are typing or resize the selection box. You can also increase or decrease the vertical distance between two lines of text. The insertion point indicates where text will appear when you type. To place the insertion point into your text, move the pointer arrow over the text—the pointer changes to an I-beam to indicate that you can click and then type.

SEE ALSO

See "Inserting Symbols and AutoText" on page 109 for information on inserting symbols and special characters.

SEE ALSO

See "Creating Bulleted and Numbered Lists" on page 98 for information on changing the bullet style.

Enter Text into a Placeholder

1. In Slide view, click the text placeholder if it isn't already selected.

2. Type the text you want to enter.

3. Click outside the text object to deselect the object.

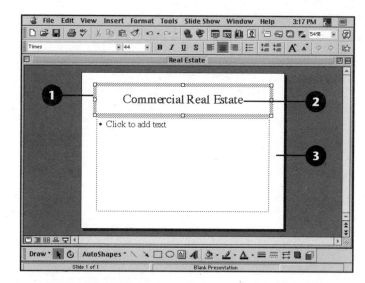

Insert Text

1. To insert text between two existing words, click between the words.

2. Type the text.

SEE ALSO

See "Formatting Text for Emphasis" on page 82 for information on formatting your text.

SEE ALSO

See "Displaying Rulers" on page 86 and "Setting Paragraph Tab" on page 87 for information on using rulers and setting tabs.

Enter Bulleted Text

1. In Slide view, click the bulleted text placeholder.

2. Type the first bulleted item.

3. Press Return. PowerPoint automatically bullets the next line.

4. If necessary, press Tab to indent the text.

5. Type the next bulleted item, and continue until you have completed the list.

   Do not press Return after the last list item.

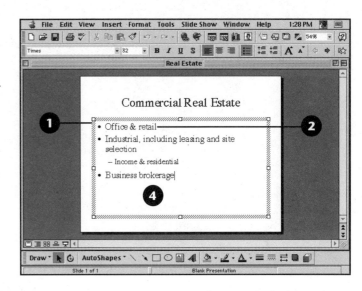

Adjust Paragraph Spacing

1. Click anywhere in the paragraph you want to adjust.

2. Click the Increase Paragraph Spacing or the Decrease Paragraph Spacing buttons on the Formatting toolbar to increase or decrease the vertical distance between paragraphs.

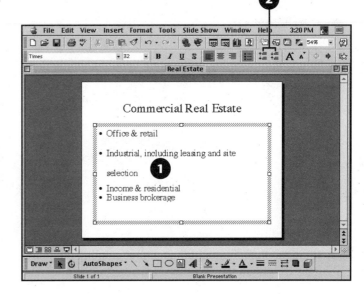

Developing an Outline

If you created your presentation using one of the AutoContent Wizards, PowerPoint generates an outline automatically. If you prefer to develop your own outline, you can create a blank presentation, and then switch to Outline view and type in your outline from scratch. In Outline view, you can add new slides and change the indent levels for slide titles and slide text. If you want to use an existing outline from another document, such as a Microsoft Word document, make sure it is set up using outline heading styles. You can then bring the outline into PowerPoint, and PowerPoint creates slide titles, subtitles, and bulleted lists based on those styles.

Outline View button

Enter Text in Outline View

1. In Outline view, click to position the insertion point where you want the text to appear.

2. Type the text you want to enter, pressing Return after each line.

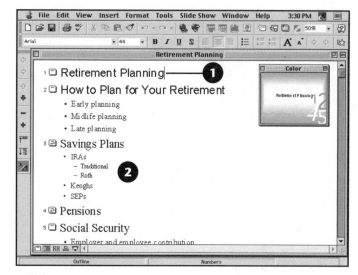

Add a Slide in Outline View

1. In Outline view, click at the end of the previous slide text.

2. Click the Insert New Slide button on the Standard toolbar, or press Option+Return to insert a slide using the existing slide layout.

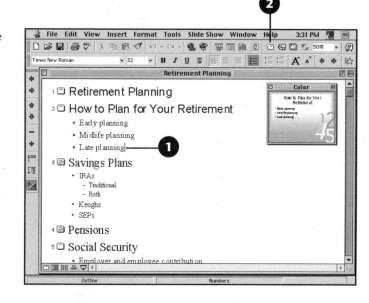

Change the Indent Level

(1) In Slide or Outline view, click anywhere in the line you want to indent.

(2) Click the Promote button or press Tab to move the line out one level (to the left).

(3) Click the Demote button or press Shift+Tab to move the line in one level (to the right).

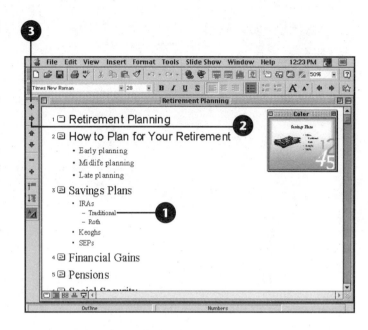

Insert an Outline from Another Application

(1) Click the Insert menu, and then click Slides From Outline.

(2) Locate and then click the file containing the outline you want to insert.

(3) Click Insert.

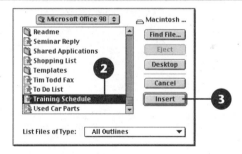

11

Rearranging Slides

You can instantly rearrange slides in Outline view or Slide Sorter view. You can use either the Move Up or Move Down button to move selected slides up or down through the outline, or you can use the Cut and Paste buttons to first cut the slides you want to move and then paste them in the new location. Outline view also lets you collapse the outline down to its major points so you can more easily see its structure. A horizontal line appears below a collapsed slide in Outline view.

TIP

Use Slide Sorter view to rearrange your slides quickly. *A vertical bar appears next to the slide you are moving as you drag a slide in Slide Sorter view. It indicates where the slide will drop when you release the mouse button.*

Rearrange Slides in Outline View

(1) Click the Outline View button.

(2) Click the slide icon of the slide or slides you want to move.

(3) Click the Move Up button to move the slide up or the Move Down button to move the slide down. Repeat until the slide is where you want it.

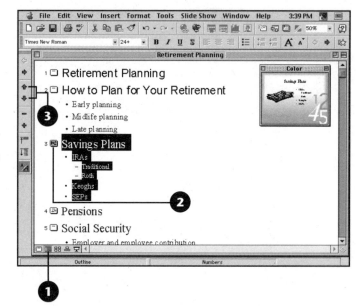

Rearrange Slides in Slide Sorter View

(1) Click the Slide Sorter View button.

(2) Click the slide you want to move, and then drag it to a new location. Release the mouse button when the slide is in the correct position.

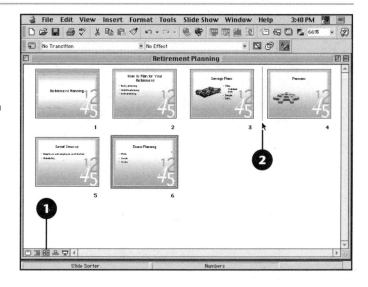

Collapse button

Expand button

Collapse All button

Expand All button

Collapse and Expand Slides in Outline View

◆ In Outline view, click the Collapse button to collapse the selected slide or slides.

◆ Click the Expand button to expand the selected slide or slides.

◆ Click the Collapse All button to collapse all slides.

◆ Click the Expand All button to expand all slides.

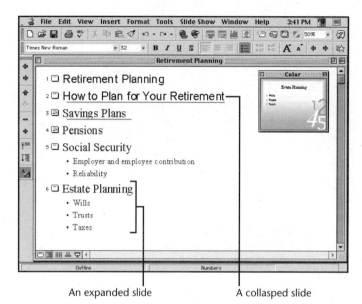

An expanded slide   A collasped slide

Move a Slide using Cut and Paste

1 In Outline or Slide Sorter view, select the slide or slides you want to move.

2 Click the Cut button on the Standard toolbar.

3 Click in the new location.

4 Click the Paste button on the Standard toolbar.

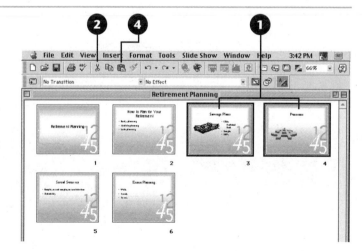

11

Controlling Slide Appearance with Masters

If you want an object, such as a company logo or clip art, to appear on every slide in your presentation, you can place it on the slide master. You can also hide the object from any slide you want. However, you can also create unique slides that don't follow the format of the masters. If you change your mind, you can easily restore a master format to a slide you altered. As you make changes to the master, you might find it helpful to view a miniature of the slide using the Slide Miniature window.

Include an Object on Every Slide

1 Click the View menu, point to Master, and then click Slide Master.

2 Add the object you want and fine-tune its size and placement.

3 Click Close on the Master toolbar.

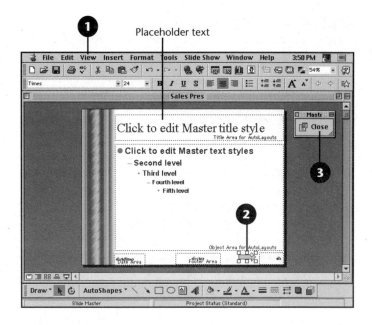

Placeholder text

Hide Master Background Objects on a Slide

1 Display the slide whose background object you want to hide.

2 Click the Format menu, and then click Background.

3 Click the Omit Background Graphics From Master check box to select it.

4 Click Apply for the current slide or click Apply To All for all slides.

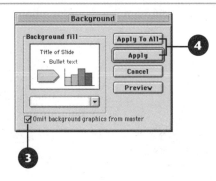

Slide Layout buton

Reapply the Master to a Changed Slide

1. Display the changed slide in Slide view.

2. Click the Slide Layout button on the Standard toolbar.

3. Click Reapply.

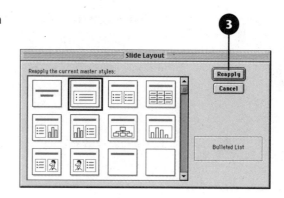

View a Miniature

1. Click the View menu, and then click Slide Miniature.

2. When you're done, click the Close box in the Slide Miniature window.

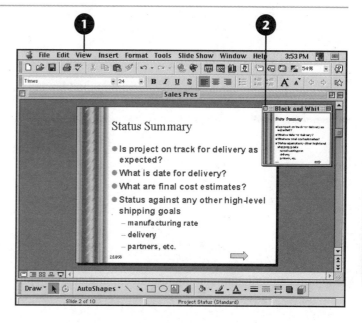

11

Applying a Color Scheme

You can apply a color scheme to an individual slide or to all the slides in a presentation. Each template offers one or more standard color schemes from which to choose, and you can also create your own color schemes, and then save them so you can apply them to other slides and even other presentations. You might like a certain color scheme, all except for one or two colors. You can change an existing color scheme and apply your changes to the entire presentation or just to a few slides. Once you change a color scheme, you can add it to your collection of color schemes so that you can make it available to any slide in the presentation.

Choose a Color Scheme

1. Click the Format menu, and then click Slide Color Scheme.

2. If necessary, click the Standard tab to view the available color schemes.

3. Click the color scheme you want.

4. Click Apply to apply the color scheme to the slide you are viewing, or click Apply To All to apply the color scheme to the entire presentation.

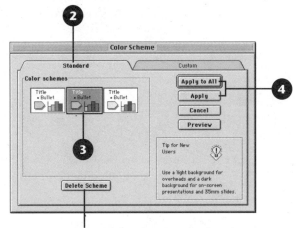

Click to delete the selected color scheme.

Customize a Color Scheme

1. Click the Format menu, and then click Slide Color Scheme.

2. Select the color scheme you want to customize.

3. Click the Custom tab.

4. Click the color box with the color you want to change.

5. Click Change Color.

6. Click the new color you want, and then click OK.

7. If necessary, click Add As Standard Scheme.

8. Click Apply or Apply To All.

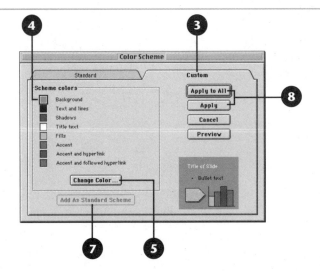

"I really like this color scheme—I'd like to apply it to a different slide."

Apply the Color Scheme of One Slide to Another

1. Click the Slide Sorter View button.

2. Click the slide with the color scheme you want to apply.

3. Click the Format Painter button on the Formatting toolbar once to apply the color scheme to one slide, or double-click to apply the color scheme to multiple slides.

4. Select the slide or slides to which you want to apply the color scheme. This can be in the current presentation or in another open presentation.

5. If you are applying the scheme to more than one slide, click the Format Painter button again to cancel Format Painter. If you are applying the scheme to only one slide, Format Painter cancels automatically.

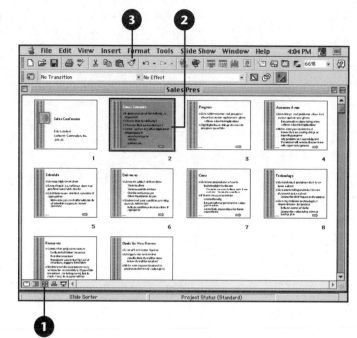

11

Printing a Presentation

You can print all elements of your presentation—the slides, the Outline view, the notes, and handouts—in either color or black and white. The Print dialog box offers standard Macintosh features, giving you the options to print multiple copies, specify ranges, access printer properties, and print to a file.

Print a Presentation

1. Click the File menu, and then click Print.
2. Click the Printer pop-up menu, and then select the printer you want.
3. Specify the copies, pages and page source you want.
4. Click the pop-up menu, and then select Microsoft PowerPoint.
5. Click the Print What pop-up menu, and then select what you want to print.
6. Click Print.

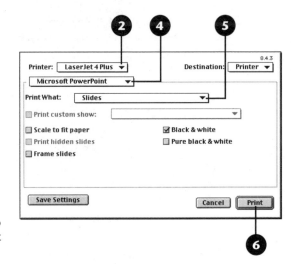

Print Outline View

1. Click the Outline View button.
2. Display the outline exactly like you want the page to print.
3. Click the File menu, and then click Print.
4. Click the pop-up menu, and then select Microsoft PowerPoint.
5. Click the Printer What pop-up menu, and then select Outline View.
6. Click OK.

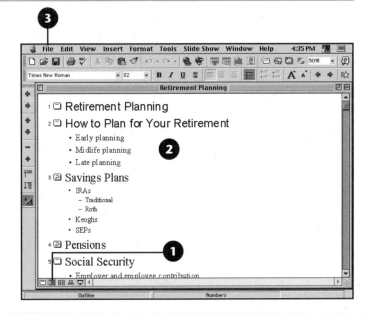

12

Designing a Presentation with PowerPoint 98

Although well-illustrated slides can't make up for a lack of content, you have a much better chance of capturing your audience's attention if your slides are vibrant and visually interesting. You can easily enhance a slide by adding a graph, a chart, or a picture—one of your own or one of the hundreds that come with Office 98. If you have the appropriate hardware, such as a sound card and speakers, you also might want to include sound files and video clips in your presentation.

Microsoft PowerPoint 98 also lets you create custom slide shows that can include special features, such as visual, sound, and animation effects. For example, you can program special *transitions,* or actions, between slides. You can also control how each element of the slide is introduced to the audience using *animations.* You can add *action buttons* to your presentation that the presenter can click to activate a hyperlink and jump instantly to another slide in the presentation. A PowerPoint presentation can really come alive with the proper use of narration and music. With PowerPoint you can record a narration and insert it directly into your slide show.

Adding a Header and Footer

Header and footer information appears on every slide except the title slide. It often includes information such as the presentation title, slide number, date, and name of the presenter. You use the masters to place header and footer information on your slides, handouts, or notes pages. Make sure your header and footer doesn't make your presentation look cluttered. The default font size of this information is usually small enough to minimize distraction, but you might want to experiment with header and footer font size and placement to make sure.

SEE ALSO

See "Adding and Modifying Media Clips" on page 42 for information on inserting and modifying clip art.

Add a Header and Footer

1. Click the View menu, and then click Header And Footer.

2. Click the Slide or Notes And Handouts tab.

3. Select the Header or Footer check box, and then fill in the information you want.

4. If you want, click to select the Date And Time or the Slide Number check box.

5. Click Appy to apply to the current slide, or click Apply To All to apply to all slides.

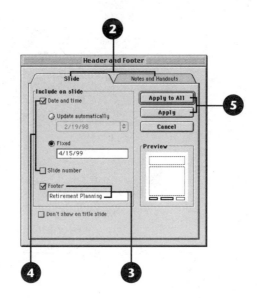

Change the Look of a Header or Footer

1. Click the View menu, point to Master, and then click the master you want to change.

2. Select the header or footer placeholder you want to change.

3. Move, resize, or change the text attributes of the placeholder.

4. Click Close on the Master toolbar.

Preparing Speaker Notes and Handouts

Every slide has a corresponding *notes page* that displays a reduced image of the slide and a text placeholder into which you can enter speaker's notes. Once you have created speaker's notes, you can reference the notes pages as you give your presentation, either from a printed copy or from your computer. Besides adding header and footer information, you can customize your notes pages and handouts by formatting the corresponding master. For handouts, you can specify how many slides you want per page.

TIP

Use Page Setup to change slide numbering. *To change the start page number, click the File menu, click Page Setup, and then enter the number you want in the Number Slides From box.*

Enter Notes in Notes Page View

1 Display the slide for which you want to enter notes.

2 Click the Notes Page View button.

3 Click the text placeholder.

4 If necessary, click the Zoom drop-down arrrow, and then increase the zoom percentage to more easily see the text you will type.

5 Type your notes.

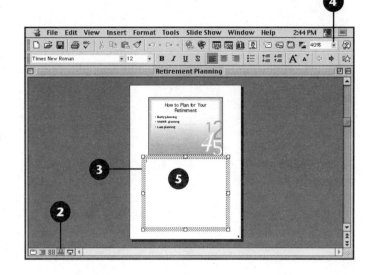

Format the Handout or Notes Master

1 Click the View menu, point to Master, and then click Handout Master or Notes Master.

2 For handouts, click one of the buttons on the Handout Master toolbar to specify how many slides you want per page.

3 Select the placeholder you want to change, and then move, resize, or change the text attributes.

4 Click Close on the Master toolbar.

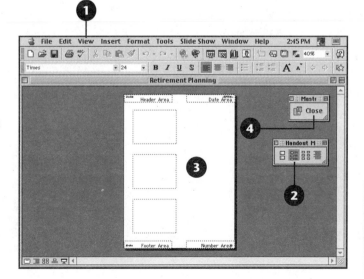

12

Inserting a Graph Chart in a Slide

You can insert an existing chart from a program such as Microsoft Excel, or you can create one from scratch using the graph program that comes with Office 98, *Microsoft Graph*. Graph uses two views to display the information that makes up a graph: the *datasheet*, a spreadsheet-like grid of rows and columns that contains your data, and the *chart*, the graphical representation of the data. A datasheet contains cells to hold your data. A *cell* is the intersection of a row and column. A group of data values from a row or column makes up a *data series*. Each data series has a unique color or pattern on the chart.

Create a Graph Chart

1 Start Microsoft Graph in one of the following ways:

- ◆ To create a graph on an existing slide, display the slide on which you want the graph to appear, and then click the Insert Chart button on the Standard toolbar.

- ◆ To create a graph on a new slide, click the Insert New Slide button on the Standard toolbar, click the Chart AutoLayout, click OK, and then double-click the chart placeholder to add the chart and datasheet.

2 Click the View Datasheet button on the Standard toolbar.

3 Replace the sample data in the datasheet with your own data.

4 Edit and format the data in the datasheet as appropriate.

5 Click the File menu, and then click Quit & Return to filename to exit Microsoft Graph.

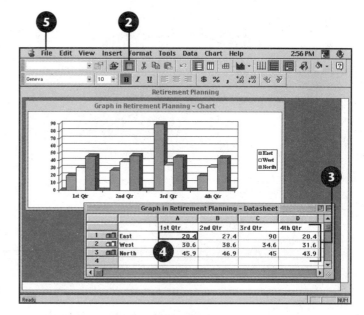

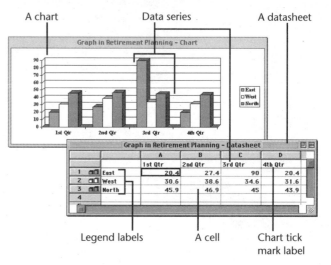

A chart — Data series — A datasheet

Legend labels — A cell — Chart tick mark label

Entering Data in Microsoft Graph

You enter graph data in the datasheet either by typing it or by inserting it from a different source. The datasheet is designed to make data entry easy, but if your data resides elsewhere, it's better not to retype it—you might make mistakes, and you would have to update your data twice. When the data that forms the bases of your chart is located elsewhere, it's usually best to link your data to the graph object.

If you type data into a cell already containing data, your entry replaces the cell contents. The cell you click is called the *active cell;* it has a thick border.

SEE ALSO

See "Viewing the Excel Window" on page 124 for more information on active cells.

Enter Data in the Datasheet

1 If necessary, double-click Microsoft Graph chart, and then click the View Datasheet button on the Standard toolbar.

2 Delete the sample data by clicking the upper left heading button to select all the cells and then pressing Del.

3 Click a cell to make it active.

4 Type the data you want entered in the cell.

5 Press Return to move the insertion point down one row, or press Tab to move the insertion point right to the next cell.

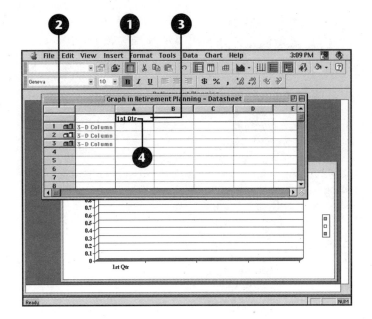

Selecting a Chart Type

Your chart is what your audience will see, so make sure to take advantage of PowerPoint's chart formatting options. You start by choosing the chart type you want. There are 18 chart types, available in 2-D and 3-D formats, and for each chart type you can choose from a variety of formats. If you want to format your chart beyond the provided formats, you can customize any chart object to your own specifications and can then save those settings so that you can apply that chart formatting to any chart you create.

TIP

Create a custom chart type. *Click the Chart menu, click Chart Type, click the Custom tab, click the User-Defined option button, click Add, type a name and description of the chart, and then click OK twice.*

Select a Chart Type

1. If necessary, click the View Datasheet button on the toolbar to close the datasheet and view the chart.

2. Click the Chart Type drop-down arrow on the Standard toolbar.

3. Click the button corresponding to the chart type you want.

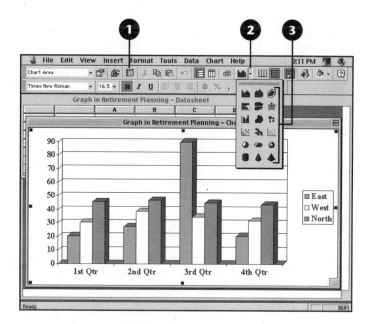

Apply a Standard or Custom Chart Type

1. Click the Chart menu, and then click Chart Type.

2. Click the Standard Types tab or the Custom Types tab.

3. Click the chart type you want.

4. If necessary, click the chart sub-type you want. *Subtypes are variations on the chart type.*

5. Click OK.

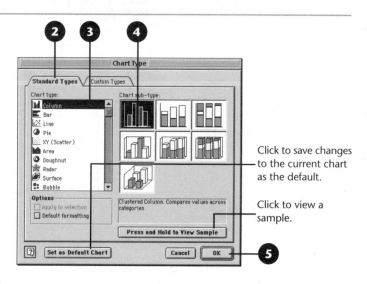

Click to save changes to the current chart as the default.

Click to view a sample.

Formatting Chart Objects

Chart objects are the individual elements that make up a chart, such as an axis, the legend, or a data series. The *plot area* is the bordered area where the data are plotted. The *chart area* is the area between the plot area and the Microsoft Graph object selection box. As with any Microsoft program, Graph treats all these elements as objects, which you can format and modify.

TIP

Use the mouse button to select a chart quickly. *You can simply click a chart object to select it, but this can be tricky if you aren't using a zoomed view since chart objects are often quite small.*

SEE ALSO

See "Enhancing a Chart" on page 154 for information on formatting and customizing a chart.

Select a Chart Object

1. Click the Chart Objects drop-down arrow on the Standard toolbar.

2. Click the chart object you want to select.

   When a chart object is selected, selection handles appear.

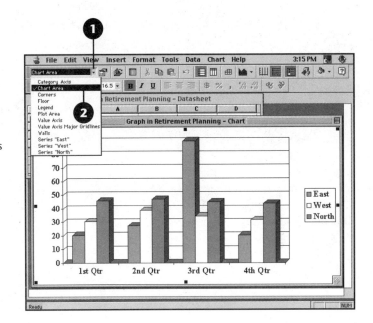

Format a Chart Object

1. Double-click the chart object you want to format, such as an axis, legend, or data series.

2. Click the appropriate tab(s) containing the options you want to change.

3. Select the options you want to apply.

4. Click OK.

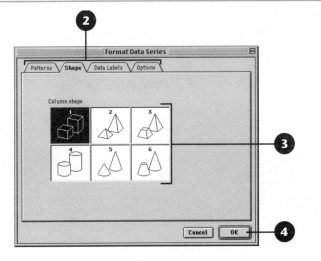

12

Creating Slide Transitions

In order to give your presentation more visual interest, you can add transitions between slides. For example, you can create a "fading out" effect so that the old slide fades out and is replaced by the new slide, or you can have one slide appear to "push" another slide out of the way. When you add a transition effect to a slide, the effect takes place between the previous slide and the selected slide. You can also add sound effects to your transitions, though you need a sound card and speakers to play these sounds.

Specify a Transition

1. View your presentation in Slide Sorter view.

2. Click the slide(s) to which you want to add a transition effect.

3. Click the Slide Transition Effects drop-down arrow on the Slide Sorter toolbar.

4. Click the transition effect you want.

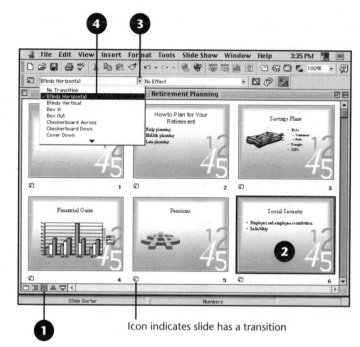

Icon indicates slide has a transition

Apply a Transition to All Slides in a Presentation

1. Click the Slide Show menu, and then click Slide Transition.

2. Click the Effect pop-up menu, and then select the transition you want.

3. Click Apply To All.

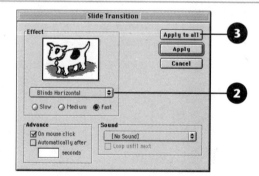

Set Transition Effect Speeds and Timing

(1) In Slide or Slide Sorter view, display or click the slide whose transition effect you want to edit.

(2) Click the Slide Show menu, and then click Slide Transition.

(3) To set speed, click the Slow, Medium, or Fast option button.

(4) To set timing, click the Automatically After check box, and then enter the time (in seconds) you want before the slide transition takes effect in slide show.

(5) Click Apply.

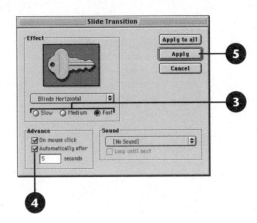

Add Sound to a Transition Effect

(1) In Slide or Slide Sorter view, display or click the slide for which you want to add a transition sound.

(2) Click the Slide Show menu, and then click Slide Transition.

(3) Click the Sound pop-up menu, and then select the sound you want.

(4) Click Apply.

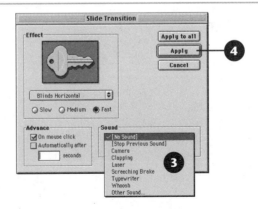

12

Adding Animation

You can use animation to introduce objects onto a slide one at a time or with special animation effects. For example, a bulleted list can appear one bulleted item at a time, or a picture or chart can fade gradually into the slide's foreground. PowerPoint supports many different kinds of animations. Some of these are called *preset animations* and are effects that PowerPoint has designed for you. Many of the preset animations contain sounds. You can also design your own *customized animations*, including your own special effects and sound elements.

TIP

Preview an animation. *In Slide view, click the Slide Show menu, and then click Animation Preview. You can click in the Slide Miniature window to preview the animation again.*

Add a Preset Animation

1. In Slide or Slide Sorter view, select the object(s) or slide(s) you want to animate.

2. Click the Slide Show menu, and then point to Preset Animation.

3. Click the animation you want.

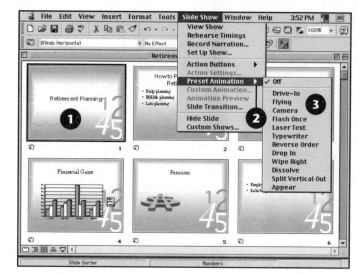

Add a Text Body Animation

1. View your presentation in Slide Sorter view.

2. Click the slide(s) to which you want to add a text body animation.

3. Click the Text Body Animation drop-down arrow on the Slide Sorter toolbar.

4. Click the text body animation you want.

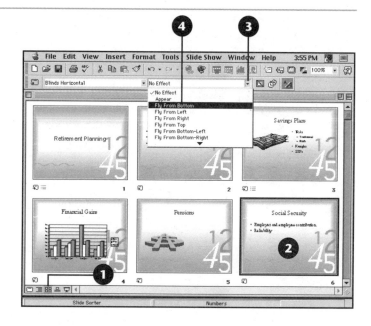

Remove animation from an object. *In the Custom Animation dialog box, click the Timing tab, click the object title you want to remove in the Animation Order box, click the Don't Animate option button, and then click OK.*

Animate a bulleted list. *Select the bulleted text object you want to animate, click the Slide Show menu, click Custom Animation, click the Grouped By check box, click the pop-up menu, select a paragraph level, and then click OK.*

Customize text animation. *Select the text object you want to animate, click the Slide Show menu, click Custom Animation, click the Introduce Text pop-up menu, select a text effect, and then click OK.*

Add Animation to an Object

1. In Slide view, click the Slide Show menu, and then click Custom Animation.

2. Click the Timing tab.

3. Select the slide object to which you want to apply an animation.

4. Click the Animate option button.

    The slide object is moved to the Animation Order box.

5. Click OK.

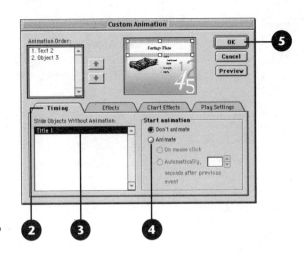

Apply a Customized Animation

1. In Slide view, click the Slide Show menu, and then click Custom Animation.

2. Click the Effects tab.

3. Click the object you want to apply an animation to.

4. Click the Animation pop-up menu, and then select the effect you want.

5. To dim text after it is animated, click the After Animation pop-up menu, and then select the color or option you want.

6. Click OK.

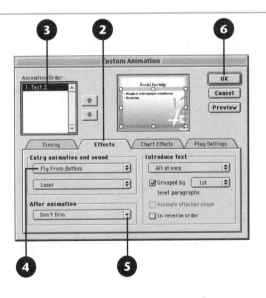

12

Adding Action Buttons

When you create a self-running presentation to be used at a kiosk, you might want a user to be able to move easily to specific slides or to a different presentation altogether. To give an audience this capability, you insert *action buttons*, which a user can click to jump to a different slide or different presentation. Clicking an action button activates a *hyperlink*, a connection between two locations in the same document or in different documents.

SEE ALSO

See "Using and Removing Hyperlinks" on page 48 for more information about hyperlinks.

Create an Action Button

1. Click the Slide Show menu, point to Action Buttons, and then click the action button you want.

2. On the slide, drag to insert and size the action button.

3. If necessary, fill out the Action Settings dialog box, and then click OK.

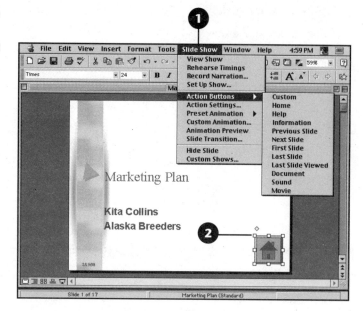

Test an Action Button

1. Click the Slide Show View button.

2. Display the slide containing your action button.

3. Click the action button.

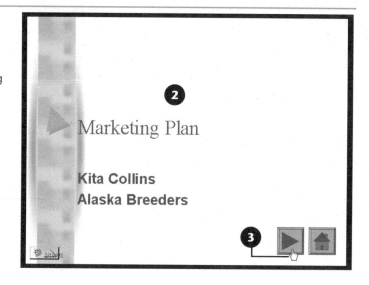

Use the Return action button to jump back to your last slide. *If you want your audience to be able to return to the slide they were previously viewing, regardless of its location in the presentation, insert the Return action button.*

Add a hyperlink to a slide object. *Select the object, click the Slide Show menu, click Action Settings, click the Hyperlink To option button, click a destination for the hyperlink, and then click OK.*

Create a Custom Action Button to Go to a Specific Slide

(1) Click the Slide Show menu, point to Action Buttons, and then click Custom.

(2) Drag to insert and size the action button on the slide.

(3) Click the Hyperlink To option button, click the pop-up menu, and then select Slide.

(4) Select the slide you want the action button to jump you to.

(5) Click OK and then click OK again.

(6) Control-click the action button, and then click Add Text.

(7) Type the name of the slide the action button points to.

(8) Click outside the action button to deselect it.

(9) Run the slide show and test the action button.

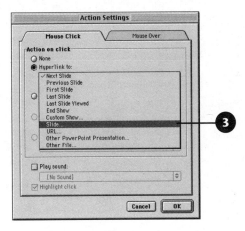

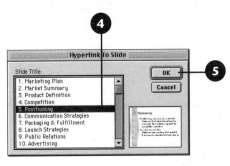

Creating a Custom Slide Show

If you plan to show a slide show to more than one audience, or you use a show regularly for different audiences, you don't have to create a separate slide show for each audience. Instead, you can create a *custom slide show* that allows you to specify which slides from the presentation you will use and the order in which they will appear.

Create a Custom Slide Show

(1) Click the Slide Show menu, and then click Custom Shows.

(2) Click New.

(3) Type a name for the custom slide show.

(4) Click the slides you want to include in the show in the order you want to present them, and then click Add.

(5) Click OK.

(6) Click Close.

List of custom slide shows for this presentation

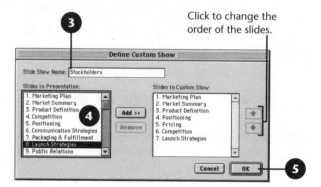

Click to change the order of the slides.

Show a Custom Slide Show

(1) Click the Slide Show menu, and then click Custom Shows.

(2) Click the custom slide show you want to run.

(3) Click Show.

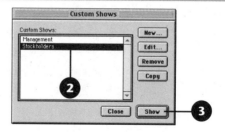

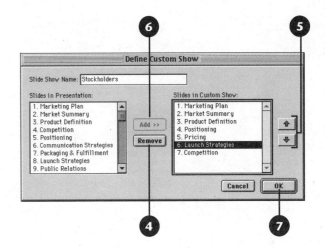

Remove a custom slide show. *To remove a custom show, click the custom slide show you want to remove in the Custom Shows dialog box, and then click the Remove button.*

Create a custom slide show from an existing one. *To create a custom slide show that is similar to an existing custom show, click the existing custom show in the Custom Shows dialog box, and then click the Copy button. A new custom show is created named Copy Of <Existing Show>. Click the Edit button to edit the copy, and give the new custom slide show its own name.*

Print a custom show. *Click the File menu, and then click Print. Click the Custom Show pop-up menu. Select the custom slide show you want to print. If applicable, set other print settings, and then click OK.*

Edit a Custom Slide Show

1. Click the Slide Show menu, and then click Custom Shows.

2. Click the show you want to edit.

3. Click the Edit button.

4. To remove a slide from the show, click the slide in the Slides In Custom Show list box, and then click Remove.

5. To move a slide up or down in the show, click the slide in the Slides In Custom Show list box, and then click the Up arrow or Down arrow button.

6. To add a slide, click the slide in the Slides In Presentation list box, and then click Add. The slide appears at the end of the Slides In Custom Show list box.

7. Click OK.

8. Click Close.

12

Presenting a Slide Show

In Slide Show view, you advance to the next slide by clicking the mouse button or pressing the Return key on your keyboard. In addition to those basic navigational techniques, PowerPoint provides keyboard shortcuts that can take you to the beginning, end, or any particular slide in your presentation. You can also use the navigation commands on the pop-up menu to access slides in custom slide shows. In a slide show, you can turn your mouse pointer into a pen, capable of highlighting and circling your key points. Marks you make on a slide with the pen during a slide show are not permanent.

TIP

Set up a continuously running slide show. *Click the Slide Show menu, click Set Up Show, click the Loop Continuously Until 'Esc' check box, and then click OK.*

Navigate a Slide Show

Refer to the adjacent table for information on how to navigate a slide show.

SLIDE SHOW NAVIGATION CONTROLS	
Action	**Result**
Mouse click or press Return	Go to the next slide
Command+click	Go to the previous slide
Press N or Page Down	Go to the next slide
Press P or Page Up	Go to the previous slide
Press slide number+Return	Go to slide number
Press Esc	Stop a slide show
Command+P	Change the pointer to a pen
Press E	Erase on-screen annotations
Command+A	Change the pen to a pointer
Press Help in slide show	Display a list of controls

Present a Slide Show

① Click the Slide Show button.

② Move the mouse pointer, and then click the pop-up menu in the left corner.

③ To go to a specific slide, point to Go, point to By Title or Custom Show, and then click the slide or slide show you want.

To use the pen, click Pen. Press the E key to erase the screen. When you're done, click the pop-up menu, and then click Arrow.

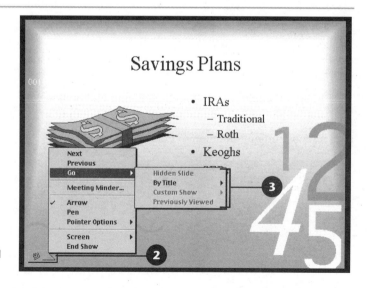

13

Sharing Information Between Office 98 Programs

One of the most helpful aspects of Microsoft Office 98 is its ability to share information between programs. This means you can create and store information in the program that works best for that type of information, yet move that same information to another program for a specific purpose or presentation. Consider the following example. Sarah coordinates her local school district's soccer teams. She needs to send out monthly newsletters that show the scheduled dates and times for practices and games. Every month Sarah writes a form letter to the players using Word, imports the upcoming schedule from Excel, and then creates a presentation for the monthly meeting using PowerPoint. Sarah also sends the presentation file to her boss for review using Outlook Express.

This is just one scenario. As you work with Office 98 programs, you'll find many ways you'll want to share information between them.

Sharing Information Between Programs

Microsoft Office 98 can convert data or text from one format to another using a technology known as *Object Linking and Embedding* (OLE). OLE allows you to move text or data between programs in much the same way as you move them within a program. The familiar cut-and-paste and drag-and-drop methods work between programs and documents just as they do within a document. In addition, all Office programs have special ways to move information from one program to another, including importing, exporting, embedding, linking, publishing, subscribing, and hyperlinking.

Importing and Exporting

Importing and exporting information are two sides of the same coin. *Importing* copies a file created with the same or another program into your open file. The information becomes part of your open file, just as if you created it in that format, although formatting and program-specific information such as formulas can be lost. *Exporting* converts a copy of your open file into the file type of another program. In other words, importing brings information into your open document, while exporting moves information from your open document into another program file.

Embedding

Embedding inserts a copy of a file created in one program into a file created in another program. Unlike imported files, you can edit the information in embedded files with the same commands and toolbar buttons used to create the original file. The original file is called the *source file*, while the file in which it is embedded is called the *destination file*. Any changes you make to an embedded object appear only in the destination file; the source file remains unchanged.

Linking

Linking displays information from one file (the source file) in a file created in another program (the destination file). You can view and edit the linked object from either the source file or the destination file. The changes are stored in the source file but also appear in the destination file as well. As you work, Office 98 updates the linked object to ensure you always work with the most current information available. Office 98 keeps track of all the drive, folder, and filename information for a source file. But, if you move or rename the source file, the link between files will be broken.

Once the link is broken, the information in the destination file becomes embedded rather than linked. In other words, changes to one copy of the file will no longer affect the other.

TERM	DEFINITION
source program	The program that created the original object.
source file	The file that contains the original object.
destination program	The program that created the document into which you are inserting the object.
destination file	The file into which you are inserting the object.

Publishing

Publishing saves a section of a document as an edition that you or others can use in other documents, such as a PowerPoint presentation or a Microsoft Word document. A *publisher* is the source document that creates an edition. The *edition* is linked to the source document, so that whenever the original is changed, the changes are reflected in the edition. If you decide you no longer need to update the information in an edition, you can cancel the publisher. The link from the publisher to the edition is removed, but other users can still subscribe to the edition.

Subscribing

Subscribing inserts a copy of the edition, an object published by another source document,in the destination document. Once you have inserted an edition into the subscriber, updates received by the edition are automatically sent to the subscriber. All editions are initially set to have automatic links. You can change a linked edition in a destination document from automatic to manual so you can control when the information is updated. With a manually linked edition, an update from the source document is not made until you request it. You might find that you no longer have access to a publisher or that you don't need to receive updated information from an edition. You can cancel the subscriber, and then you are free to edit the information from the edition in the destination document.

Hyperlinking

The newest way to share information between programs is hyperlinks—a term borrowed from World Wide Web technology. A *hyperlink* is an object (either colored, underlined text or a graphic) you click to jump to a different location in the same document or a different document. (See "Creating Internet Documents with Office 98" on page 45 for more information about creating and navigating hyperlinks in Office documents.)

Importing and Exporting Files

When you *import* data, you insert a copy of a file (from the same or another program) into an open document. When you *export* data, you save an open document in a new format so that it can be opened in an entirely different program. For example, you might import an Excel worksheet into a Word document to create a one page report with text and a table. Or you might want to save the Excel worksheet as an earlier version of Excel so someone else can edit, format, and print it.

Import a File from the Same or Another Program

(1) Click where you want to insert the imported file.

(2) Click the Insert menu and then click File (in Word) or Slide From File (in PowerPoint).

(3) Click the List Files Of Type pop-up menu, and then click Readable Files.

(4) If necessary, click the pop-up menu, and then select the drive and folder that contains the file you want to import.

(5) Select the file you want to import.

(6) Click Insert.

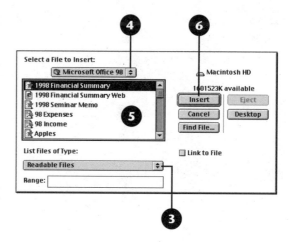

Use copy and paste to export information. *If you want to move only part of a file into your document, just copy the information you want to insert, and then paste the information in the file where you want it to appear.*

See "Saving a File" on page 12 for more information about saving a file as another file type.

Export a File to Another Program

1 Click the File menu, and then click Save As.

2 If necessary, click the pop-up menu, and then select the drive and folder in which you want to save the file.

3 Click the Save File As Type pop-up menu, and then select the type of file you want to save the file as.

4 If necessary, type a new name for the file.

5 Click Save.

You can now edit the file from within the new program.

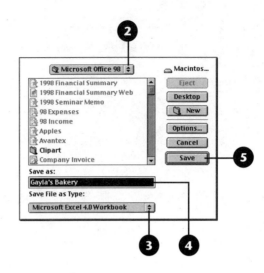

Embedding and Linking Information

Embedding inserts a copy of one document into another. Once data is embedded, you can edit it using the menus and toolbars of the program in which it was created (that is, the source program). *Linking* displays information stored in one document (the source file) into another (the destination file). You can edit the linked object from either file, although changes are stored in the source file.

TIP

Change an object from linked to embedded. *If you break the link between an linked object and its source file, it becomes merely embedded. To break a link, open the linked file, click the Edit menu, click Links, and then click the link you want to break. Finally, click Break Link, and then click Yes.*

Embed an Object from a File

1. Click where you want to embed the object.

2. Click the Insert menu, and then click Object.

3. Click From File or the Create From File option button.

4. Select the file you want to embed as an object.

5. Click Insert.

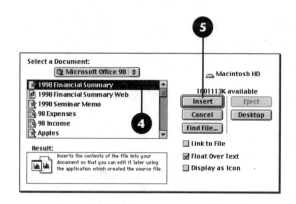

Embed a New Object

1. Click where you want to embed the object.

2. Click the Insert menu, and then click Object.

3. Click the Create New tab or Create New option button.

4. Click the type of object you want to create.

5. Click OK.

6. Enter the necessary information in the new object using its program commands.

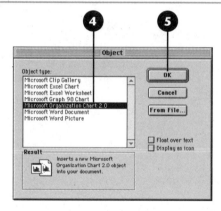

Create a travel budget. *In Excel, create a worksheet with columns showing the actual expenses for a trip for two, three, and four people per room. In Word, write a description of the trip, and then link the travel budget below the description. Distribute the Word document to prospective travelers. Update the information as needed from either the Word or Excel file.*

Link an Object Between Programs

1. Click where you want to link the object.

2. Click the Insert menu, and then click Object.

3. Click From File or the Create From File option button.

4. Click the Link To File check box to select it.

5. Select the file you want to link as an object.

6. Click OK or Insert.

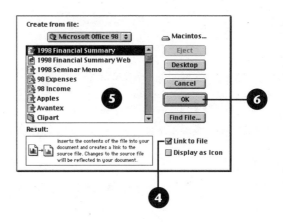

Edit an Embedded or Linked File

1. Double-click the linked or embedded object you want to edit to display the source program's menus and toolbars.

2. Edit the object as usual using the source program's commands.

3. When you're finished, click the File menu, and then click Close & Return or Quit & Return.

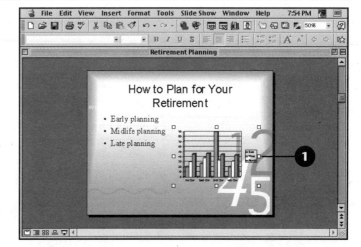

Publishing and Subscribing to an Edition

A *publisher* is the source document that you use to create an edition. When you create a publisher, you are saving a section of a document as an *edition* that you or others can use in other documents. The edition is linked to the source document, so that whenever the original is changed, the changes are reflected in the edition. Once you have published an edition, you can subscribe to the edition. When you *subscribe* to an edition, you insert a copy of the edition into your document. Once you have inserted an edition into the subscriber, updates received by the edition are automatically sent to the subscriber.

Publish an Edition

1. Select the information you want to publish.
2. Click the Edit menu, point to Publishing, and then click Create Publisher.
3. Type the name of the new edition.
4. Select a location in which to store the edition file.
5. Click Publish.

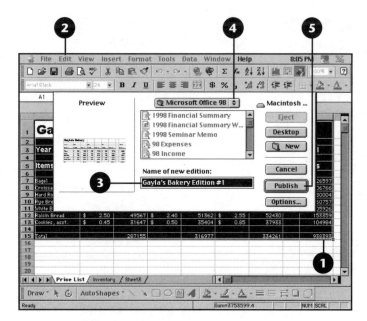

Subscribe to an Edition

1. Select the location where you want to place the edition.
2. Click the Edit menu, point to Publishing, and then click Subscribe To.
3. Locate the edition file you want to subscribe to.
4. Select the edition file you want to subscribe to.
5. Click Subscribe.

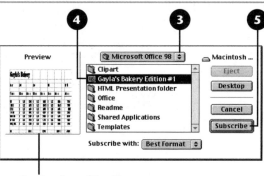

Preview the edition file.

SEE ALSO

See "Sharing Information Between Programs" on page 220 for more information about publishing and subscribing to an edition.

"How do I cancel a publisher or subscriber?"

Change Publisher or Subscriber Options

1 Open the file with the published or subcribed edition.

2 In Excel, click the Edit menu, click Links, select the edition, and then click Options.

In Word, click the Edit menu, point to Publishing, and then click Publisher Options or Subscriber Options.

3 To cancel a publisher or subscriber, click Cancel Publisher or Cancel Subscriber.

4 To change how the edition updates, click one of the update option buttons.

5 Click OK.

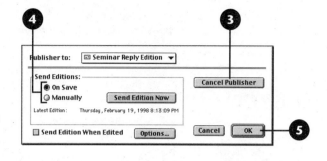

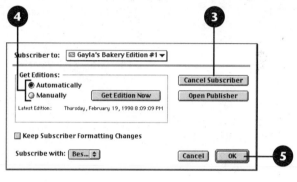

13

Creating Word Documents with Excel Data

A common pairing of Office programs combines Word and Excel. As you write a sales report, explain a budget, or create a memo showing distribution of sales, you'll often want to add worksheet data and charts to your text. Instead of re-creating the Excel data in Word, you can insert all or part of the data or chart into your Word document.

Insert an Excel Worksheet Range into a Word Document

(**1**) Click in the Word document where you want to copy the Excel range.

(**2**) Click the Insert menu, and then click File.

(**3**) Click the pop-up menu, and then select the drive and folder that contains the workbook you want to copy.

(**4**) If necessary, click the List Files Of Type pop-up menu, and then select Readable Files.

(**5**) Click the filename of the workbook you want to copy.

(**6**) Click Insert.

(**7**) Click the Open Document In Workbook pop-up menu, and then select the workbook you want.

(**8**) Click the Name Or Cell Range pop-up menu, and select the range you want to copy.

(**9**) Click OK.

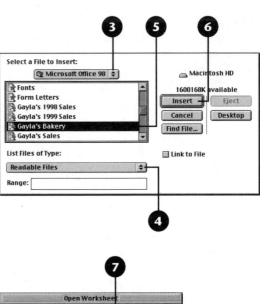

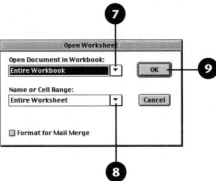

Import Excel data as a picture. *To save disk space, you can insert Excel data as a picture. Data inserted this way becomes a table that you cannot edit. Select the data you want to import, press the Shift key as you click the Edit menu, and then click Copy Picture. In the Copy Picture dialog box, click OK. Click in the Word document where you want to insert the picture, and then click the Paste button on the Standard toolbar. Drag the picture borders until it's easy to read.*

Create a new Excel worksheet directly in Word document. *With the insertion point where you want the worksheet, click the Insert MS Excel Worksheet button on the Standard toolbar, drag to select the number of rows and columns you want, type the data and format the worksheet as needed, and then click outside the worksheet to return to the Word window. When you save the file, the worksheet becomes embedded in the Word document.*

Embed an Excel Chart in Word

(1) Open the Excel workbook that contains the chart you want to use.

(2) Click the Excel chart you want to embed to select it.

(3) Click the Copy button on the Standard toolbar.

(4) Click in the Word document where you want to embed the chart.

(5) Click the Paste button on the Standard toolbar.

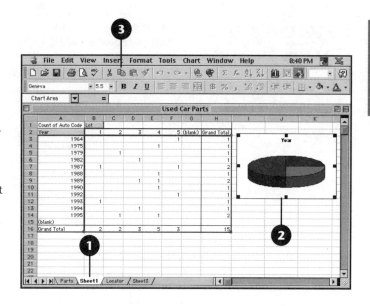

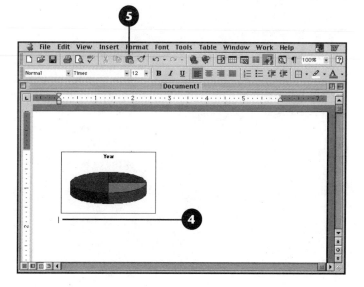

Creating a PowerPoint Presentation with Word Text

PowerPoint presentations are based on outlines, which you can create either using PowerPoint or the more extensive outlining tools in Word. You can import any Word document into PowerPoint, although only paragraphs tagged with heading styles become part of the slides. You can also copy any table you created in Word to a slide.

SEE ALSO

See "Applying a Style" on page 95 and "Creating and Modifying a Style" on page 96 for more information about using heading styles in Word.

Create PowerPoint Slides from a Word Document

1. Create a Word document with heading styles, and then close the Word document.

2. In PowerPoint, click the Open button on the Standard toolbar.

3. Click the List Files Of Type pop-up menu, and then select All Outlines.

4. Click the pop-up menu, and then locate the Word file you want to use.

5. Double-click the Word document filename.

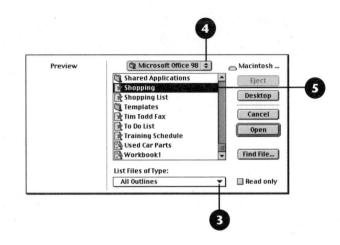

Embed a Word Table in a Slide

1. Click in the Word table you want to use in a slide.

2. Click the Table menu, and then click Select Table.

3. Click the Copy button on the Word Standard toolbar.

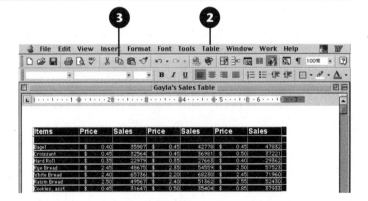

④ Display the PowerPoint slide where you want to insert the Word table.

⑤ Click the Paste button on the PowerPoint Standard toolbar.

⑥ Drag a handle to resize the embedded table.

⑦ Double-click the table to display Word's menus and toolbars, and edit the table using the usual Word commands.

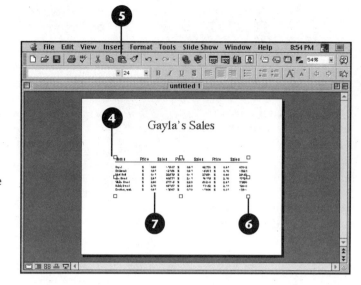

Create a Word Document from a PowerPoint Presentation

① Open the PowerPoint presentation you want to use as a Word document.

② Click the File menu, point to Send To, and then click Microsoft Word.

Word starts and opens the presentation as a Word document.

③ Edit the text using the usual Word commands.

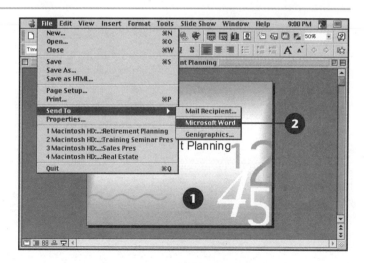

Sending Files in E-Mail Messages

When you want others to receive a copy of an Office 98 file, you can send the file through e-mail. You can also route a file through e-mail, rather than send it, when you want others to review a copy of it online. You can send the file to one recipient after another, so that each recipient can see the previous revisions, or to all recipients at once. As the file is routed, you can track its status. After all of the recipients have reviewed the file, it is automatically returned to you.

Send a File to Others in an E-mail Message

1. Open the file you want to send.

2. Click the File menu, point to Send To, and then select Mail Recipient. If necessary, click OK.

   Your default e-mail program (such as Microsoft Outlook Express) opens, displaying a new e-mail message window with an attached file.

3. Click in the To box, and then enter an e-mail address.

4. Click in the Subject box, and then enter the subject text.

5. Click in the message box, and then enter message text.

   You can format the text like you would any other text.

6. Click Send on the toolbar.

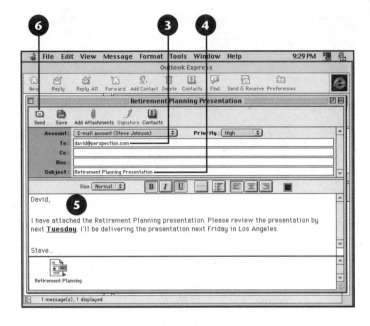

Reading and Replying to E-Mail Messages

Mail can be sent to you at anytime. Before you can retrieve your e-mail, you need to connect to the Internet. Once you are connected, you can send and receive e-mail. New messages appear in the Inbox along with any messages you haven't yet stored elsewhere or deleted. Unread messages appear in bold text, while previously read messages appear in normal text. Once you have read a message, you can reply to the author and other recipients.

Mail button

TIP

Divert incoming e-mail to folders. *Click the Tools menu, click Inbox Rules, click New Rule, set criteria for incoming messages, and then click OK.*

Open and Read a Message

1. Double-click the Mail icon on the desktop and connect to the Internet.

2. Click the Send & Receive button on the toolbar.

3. Click Inbox in the folder list.

4. Click a message to display it in the Preview pane, or double-click a message to open it up in its own window.

Reply to a Message

1. Open the message you want to reply to.

2. Click the Reply or Reply All button on the toolbar.

3. Type your message and attach any files you want to send.

4. Click the Send button on the toolbar, or click the File menu, and then click Send Later.

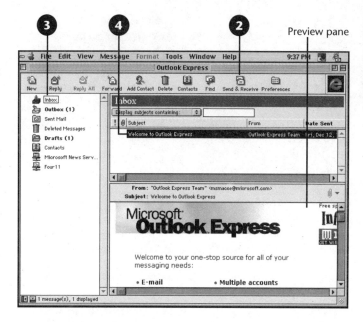

Preview pane

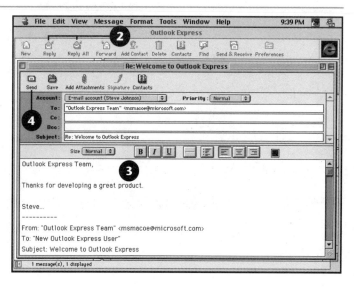

Managing E-Mail Messages

One problem that can arise as you receive e-mail is an overabundance of messages in your Inbox. To help you manage your mail messages, Outlook Express provides a way to delete messages, and move messages to other folders and subfolders. Storing messages in other folders and deleting unwanted messages make it easier to see the new messages you receive. You can move a message into another folder quickly and easily: simply, drag the message to the folder you want in the folder list.

You can also add and edit contact information, including names and e-mail addresses to keep the informatin current.

TIP

Add a new folder to the folder list. *Click the File menu, point to New, and then click Folder or Subfolder.*

Delete Unwanted E-Mail Messages

1. In Outlook Express, click the folder containing the messages you want to delete.

2. Select the message(s) you want to delete.

3. Click the Delete button on the toolbar.

4. Click Deleted Messages in the folder list.

5. Click the Edit menu, and then click Empty Deleted Messages.

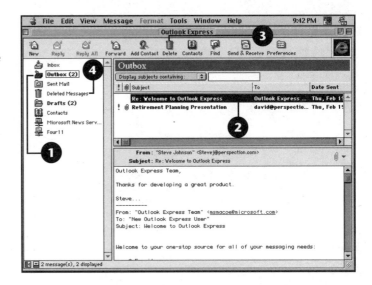

Add or Edit a Contact to the Address Book

1. In Oulook Express, click Contacts in the folder list.

2. To add a contact, click New on the Standard toolbar.

3. To edit a contact, select the contact you want to edit, and then click Edit on the Standard toolbar.

4. Enter or edit the contact information.

5. Click Save.

6. Click the Close box.

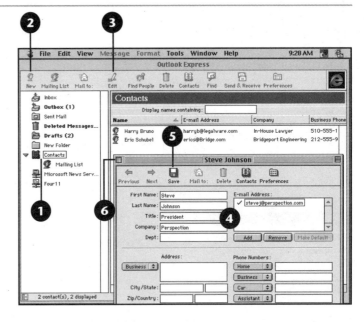

Index

arithmetic operators, 140
    order of precedence, 141
arrowhead symbol (▶), menu
    symbol, 22
arrows, styling, 39
asterisk (*), multiplication
    operator, 140
auditing Excel worksheets, 177
AutoCalculate, calculating
    with, 144
AutoComplete
    enabling for cell values, 127
    entering worksheet cell labels
        with, 126, 127
    finding Internet addresses
        with, 62
AutoContent Wizard
    (PowerPoint)
    creating presentations, 185
    for the Web, 59
AutoCorrect
    adding entries to, 33
    correcting spelling while
        typing, 32, 76
    creating exceptions to, 33
    reversing changes made
        by, 33
AutoFill (Excel), filling in data
    in worksheets, 144
AutoFilter (Excel), filtering
    records in Excel lists, 145,
    158
AutoFit (Word), adjusting table
    column widths, 117
AutoFormat (Excel), formatting
    worksheet text and
    numbers, 147
AutoLayout placeholders
    (PowerPoint), 191
AutoLayouts (in PowerPoint),
    applying to slides, 190,
    191
AutoText (in Word), inserting,
    109

AVERAGE function (Excel), 143

Background dialog box
    (PowerPoint), 198
background objects (on
    PowerPoint masters),
    hiding on slides, 198
backup copies, saving, 13
balloon help, 14
barcodes, POSTNET, printing
    on envelopes, 104
blank files, creating, 9
boldface, applying in Word, 82
bookmarks (in Word),
    inserting, 47
borders
    adding to pictures, 43
    adding to tables in Word,
        118, 120
    adding to text in Word, 120
    adding to worksheet cells,
        149
Break dialog box (Word),
    inserting page/section
    breaks, 94
brochures, creating, 41, 120, 121
Browse Arrow buttons (Word
    window), 67
Browse button (Word
    window), 67
Browse toolbar (Word), 67
browsing Word documents, 67
bulleted lists
    animating, 212, 213
    creating
        in PowerPoint, 193
        in Word, 98
    creating slides from, 193
    restyling in Word, 99
Bullets And Numbering dialog
    box (Word), 99

buttons
    column/row indicator
        buttons (in Excel
        worksheets), 136
    option buttons (in dialog
        boxes), 22
    scroll buttons (for
        worksheets), 125
    view buttons, 64, 65, 187
    See also action buttons;
        toolbar buttons; *and*
        specific buttons

calculating
    with Excel functions, 143
    using AutoCalculate, 144
capitalization, correcting, 32, 76
case, matching in Word
    searches, 74
cell contents (data)
    in Excel worksheets
        aligning, 148
        analyzing, 145, 156-64
        auditing, 177
        consolidating from
            worksheets/
            workbooks, 174-75
        creating/showing
            scenarios of, 178
        creating Word docu-
            ments with, 228-29
        editing, 128
        entering, 126-27
        filling in automatically,
            144
        importing as pictures, 229
        protecting, 164
        summarizing, 145, 160-61
    in Graph datasheets,
        entering, 207
    in Word tables

deleting, 113
    entering, 112, 113
cell formats (in Excel
    worksheets), copying,
    147
Cell Height And Width dialog
    box (Word), 117
cell references (in Excel
    worksheets), 124
    absolute, 141
    entering in formulas, 140
cells
    in Excel worksheets, 124
        active cell, 124
        adding borders to, 149
        addresses, 124, 140
        auditing, 177
        clearing, 129
        copying, 176
        copying cell formats, 147
        deleting, 129
        entering text and
            numbers into,
            126-27
        inserting, 129
        linking, 165, 176
        removing arrows from,
            177
        selecting multiple, 130-31
        See also cell contents
            (data), in Excel
            worksheets; cell
            references; ranges
    in Graph datasheets, 206
        active cell, 207
        entering data into, 207
    in Word tables
        aligning text within,
            118-19
        changing text direction
            within, 119
        clearing, 113
        entering text into, 112,
            113

formatting *continued*
    text
        in Excel worksheets, 146, 147
        with find and replace, 31, 74-75
        while typing, 83
        in Word documents, 66, 74-75, 81-104
        See also text formatting
Formatting toolbar, 24, 64
    Alignment buttons, 106
    indenting text, 88, 89
formula bar (Excel window), 124
    editing cell contents, 128
formula prefix (=), 140
formulas (in Excel worksheets), 140
    auditing, 177
    cell changes and, 129
    copying, 141
    displaying, 141
    entering, 140
    entering cell references in, 140
    using ranges/range names in, 142
    See also functions (in Excel)
fractions, entering, 32
frames (of Web pages), 61
Free Rotate button (WordArt toolbar), 41
freezing/unfreezing columns/ rows in Excel worksheets, 167
function keys. *See* F keys
functions (in Excel worksheets), 143
    calculating with, 143
    entering, 143

Genigraphics, installing, 231

GIF format, 61
grammar, correcting in Word, 76-77
Graph (Microsoft), 206
    See also under charts
graphic formats, types, 61
graphic objects. *See* objects
graphs. *See* charts
gridlines
    in Excel charts, 154
        adding, 154, 155
        major versus minor, 155
        printing worksheets with, 139, 149
    in Word tables, displaying/ hiding, 119
grouping objects, 39

handles, selection handles, 36
Handout Master, formatting, 205
handouts, adding to presentations, 205
Header And Footer toolbar (Word), 106, 107
    buttons, 108
headers
    in Excel worksheets, printing, 139
    in slides, adding/changing, 204
    in Word documents, 106
        aligning, 106, 107
        creating, 106-7
        setting margins for, 91
headings (in Word documents), as converted in PowerPoint, 231
Help, 14-17
    balloon help, 14

getting information on particular topics, 14, 15
Office Assistant, 16-17, 124, 160
hiding
    background objects on slides, 198
    gridlines, in tables in Word documents, 119
    Office programs, 20
    rulers (in Word), 86
    ScreenTips, 25
    slides in slide shows, 189
    toolbars, 24, 50
Highlight Changes dialog box (Excel), 162
highlighting (in Word documents), applying, 82, 83, 111
HTML (Hypertext Markup Language), 60
HTML documents, saving Office documents as, 60-61
Hyperlink To Slide dialog box (PowerPoint), 215
hyperlinked documents
    address list, 54
    favorites, 58
    jumping to, 45, 52, 53, 54, 58
    navigating, 45, 54-55
    reloading, 55
    See also hyperlinks; Web documents
hyperlinks, 45, 48, 221
    adding to slides, 215
    clicking, 48
    inserting, 46-47
    removing, 49
    renaming, 49
    stopping, 55
    See also action buttons
Hypertext Markup Language. *See* HTML

hyphenating Word documents, 78

importing
    Excel data as pictures, 229
    files, 220, 222
    See also inserting
Increase Indent button (Formatting toolbar), 88, 89
indenting
    paragraphs
        in PowerPoint, 195
        in Word, 88
    tables in Word documents, 117
index fields (in Excel), protecting list order with, 159
information
    exporting, 223
    getting Help on particular topics, 14, 15
    getting information about the Web, 15
    searching for information on the Web, 56
    sharing information between Office programs, 219-34
Insert Date button (Header And Footer toolbar), 108
Insert dialog box (Excel), 129
Insert File dialog box (Word), 222, 228
Insert Hyperlink dialog box, 46-47
Insert Number Of Pages button (Header And Footer toolbar), 108
Insert Outline dialog box (PowerPoint), 195

Register Today!

Return this
Microsoft® Office 98 Macintosh® Edition
At a Glance
registration card for
a Microsoft Press® catalog

U.S. and Canada addresses only. Fill in information below and mail postage-free. Please mail only the bottom half of this page.

1-57231-916-X   *MICROSOFT® OFFICE 98 MACINTOSH® EDITION*   *Owner Registration Card*
AT A GLANCE

_____
NAME

_____
INSTITUTION OR COMPANY NAME

_____
ADDRESS

_____

_____
CITY   STATE   ZIP

Microsoft®*Press*
Quality Computer Books

**For a free catalog of
Microsoft Press® products, call
1-800-MSPRESS**